Luther the Anti-Semite

Luther the Anti-Semite

A Contemporary Jewish Perspective

ALON GOSHEN-GOTTSTEIN

FORTRESS PRESS
MINNEAPOLIS

LUTHER THE ANTI-SEMITE
A Contemporary Jewish Perspective

Cover design: Rob Dewey

Print ISBN: 978-1-5064-4582-3
eBook ISBN: 978-1-5064-4583-0

The paper used in this publication meets the minimum requirements of American National Standard for Information Sciences — Permanence of Paper for Printed Library Materials, ANSI Z329.48-1984.

Manufactured in the U.S.A.

In memory of Krister Stendahl
One of my heroes

Contents

Preface

THOMAS KAUFMANN

There is something particular in the present celebration of a Jubilee of the Reformation that is different from the many other celebrations of the Reformation from the seventeenth century onward. On the occasion of the five hundredth anniversary, Luther's extremely problematic relations to the Jewish people and to Judaism stand at the center of interest. Protestant, especially Lutheran, Christians are presently very aware of the hateful texts the Wittenberg Reformer published from the later 1530s up to his last sermon, given in Eisleben on February 15, 1546, some days before his death. Intensive scholarly research has shown that from the late nineteenth century onward, several anti-Semites were devoted to Luther as their patron. During the Third Reich, high representatives of the evangelical churches in Germany and several theologians fell back on Luther's hate-filled remarks to demonstrate that Protestantism was "up to date" in relation to racial anti-Semitism.

Luther's central concern was to interpret the Old Testament as a Christian book, announcing Jesus as the savior. Nevertheless, he also adopted prejudices of an early-modern kind of anti-Semitism. Personally, for at least two decades of his life, Luther was obsessed by the fear of being poisoned by Jews. As far as we know, Luther's hatred of Jewish people had very little to do with real personal experiences but drew upon prejudices, projections, and obsessions of all kinds. All this led him to reject the Jewish people as the devil's allies, who aimed to undermine Christian life. Consequently, Luther was attractive to anti-Semites.

In the context of the preparations for the five hundredth anniversary of the Reformation, some researchers and Protestant synods have pointed out that Luther's negative attitudes to Judaism were deeply rooted in the center of his theology. We are in the position of knowing much more about Luther's life and mental disposition than we do of all of his other contemporaries. The sources are varied and include an extremely broad spectrum of academic texts, sermons, letters, table talks, and other materials. Consequently, his figure opens up perspectives on the past that allow us to reconstruct a foreign world of intolerance and hatred at the core of Western civilization. Recognizing these attitudes at the heart of our own tradition allows us to realize how long, ambivalent, and even contradictory the paths were that led to today's standards of human rights.

I am deeply impressed by the present work of Alon Goshen-Gottstein. His interpretation of the German Reformer as a model of religious intolerance, even fanaticism, has a lot to teach us about the foundations of religious intolerance. Paradoxically, seen from this perspective, Luther can actually help us to improve through an original approach to learning from the faults of a great religious figure. It is a great honor for me to contribute this preface to a highly creative and demanding piece of scholarship that will hopefully find many readers.

Thomas Kaufmann,
Göttingen,
May 2017

Introduction

When I recently mentioned to my friend Yossi, a journalist who is active in interfaith education, that I was planning a project on Martin Luther in the context of a Jewish-Christian conversation, he remarked to me: “Alon, you must be the only person who cares about a subject like this.” This might best sum up a prevalent attitude toward Luther in Jewish circles: he is not someone to be engaged; he is of little interest. The most likely explanation for the lack of interest in someone who shaped the religious and cultural landscape of Germany, Europe, and eventually most of the world is related to his attitude toward the Jews. Bluntly, Martin Luther was an anti-Semite. The point has been nuanced, contextualized, and explained. It has also been repudiated by contemporary Lutheran Churches and made the subject of an apology by all major Lutheran Churches. But the fact remains: for most Jews after the Shoah, Martin Luther is not an inviting religious personality, not someone they would wish to spend time studying, engaging, and understanding.

The present study grows out of an attempt to apply a novel perspective to Martin Luther and out of a broader approach to religious personalities under the rubric of "religious genius."[1] Through this category, it is suggested, one can identify, appreciate, and be inspired by great religious personalities of other traditions. The grammar of "religious genius," if one might call it that, allows us to describe and recognize greatness and to identify a core of spiritual greatness in outstanding religious personalities who have been transformative in their traditions. A major aspect of "religious genius" is the capacity of "religious geniuses" to inspire beyond their own native faith. Given the interest in recognizing greatness, and in view of the Reformation's anniversary, it would make sense to revisit Luther in light of this category.

This was, and remains, a project I have undertaken together with a Luther theologian, Vítor Westhelle. We had intended for this book, as a Jewish-Christian conversation, to appear on the occasion of the five hundredth anniversary of the Reformation, offering a novel dual perspective: that of "religious genius" and that of a unique Jewish-Christian conversation that seeks to explore ways Luther can be inspiring to a Jewish reader, despite all we know about his anti-Semitism. Man proposes, and two men had to adapt their plans to a reality that God provides. Health-related circumstances have forced a delay in the realization of that project. Prayer is the ultimate response, and heartfelt prayers for healing and continuing creativity for my partner are herewith offered in the hope many future projects will be realized by him. However, this unexpected complication has led to the present book as a self-standing publication that has the potential to contribute to the ongoing examination of the figure of

1. See Alon Goshen-Gottstein, *Religious Genius: Appreciating Inspiring Individuals across Traditions* (New York: Palgrave, 2017).

Luther as part of the celebrations and commemorations associated with the five hundredth anniversary.

Vítor conceived of our work beginning with a challenge that I would present to him. The challenge, coming from a Jewish scholar and a rabbi, would be how we can make sense of Luther and account for his greatness in view of his terrible views and recommendations in relation to Jews. The suggestion that the way to "Luther as religious genius" somehow passes through or must begin with a reflection on "Luther and the Jews" gave rise to thinking of this issue that extended beyond the boundaries of the study of "religious genius." Because this reflection, initially contextualized within a conversation on "religious genius," has taken on a life of its own beyond the parameters of that conversation, I have chosen to make it available as a self-standing reflection on Luther from a contemporary Jewish perspective. Its lessons and suggestions are independent of a discussion of "religious genius," even though they can, and I hope eventually also will, feed into that conversation. The present reflection on Luther as an anti-Semite is heavily informed by my own work as a Jewish thinker and interreligious activist working across multiple faith traditions in a contemporary global context. It is this broader perspective that has allowed me to recognize the broader potential that revisiting Luther's anti-Semitism has not only for Jewish-Christian (Lutheran) relations but for relations between religious of different faiths more broadly. I therefore seek to offer here a new reading of Luther as a model for a certain reality of the religious life, a reality that we can refer to, from a present-day perspective, as something going wrong in religion that finds expression in relation to the religious other. Luther's theology is particular to his time and tradition. But the broader dynamics that find expression in his writings on the Jews have wide-ranging significance, both within the reciprocal relations of Jews and Christians and, even more extensively, within the multilateral relations of different faith communities in connection to one another. In all this, Luther emerges as imperfect but nevertheless a model teacher through whom we can study how and when religion goes wrong. In offering us the example not to follow, he also does us a great service and calls us to deeper examination of ourselves. This work, then, is a new perspective on "Luther and the Jews" that does not seek to accuse, justify, or understand. Rather, based on the work of specialists in the field, it seeks to extract fundamental dynamics, recognize complex factors as these cohere into broader patterns (what I will call a model), and consider how all these serve as lessons for Jews, Christians, and others as they consider their relations with one another in today's complex reality. Luther can speak to us half a millennium later because the factors that derailed him off the course of a higher religious vision and reality continue to operate and have the potential to affect us all. Luther is a model, a warning sign, and, in significant ways, a teacher from whom we can draw important lessons, even if these are the opposite of an invitation to follow his example.

1.

Luther the Anti-Semite

Luther would have never been described by his contemporaries as an anti-Semite. The term had not yet come into existence, and the cultural and moral overtones associated with this term were not part of common discourse. In its own way, this recognition already places Luther in a different historical context, which alleviates, ever so slightly, the charges associated with anti-Semitism. If today anti-Semitism has gone in Christian eyes from being a negative attitude to being a sin,[1] in Luther's days none of the negativity associated with anti-Semitism, or a milder form of it—anti-Judaism—existed. We therefore apply criteria of later times to earlier realities.[2]

1. For Christian statements against anti-Semitism, see Franklin Sherman, ed., *Bridges: Documents of the Christian-Jewish Dialogue*, 2 vols. (New York: Paulist, 2011–14), 1:43–44, 53–54, 99–100, 174, 191–92, 267, 308; 2:145–46, 150–51, 170–73, 205, 402–9. See further John Paul II, "Address of His Holiness John Paul II to Representatives of the Jewish Community" (speech from apostolic journey to Poland and Hungary, Apostolic Nunciature of Budapest, August 18, 1991), http://tinyurl.com/y8b4ryvt; "Church in Poland Tells Catholics 'Anti-Semitism Is a Sin' and Condemns 'Indifference' of Some Christians During Holocaust," Inside-Poland.com, October 20, 2015, http://tinyurl.com/y9hfcf5u.

2. On the question of criteria and their application to Martin Luther, see Christopher J. Probst, *Demonizing the Jews: Luther and the Protestant Church in Nazi Germany* (Bloomington: Indiana University Press, 2012). Cf. Heiko A. Oberman, *The Roots of*

These criteria have a twofold value. They allow us to speak of something that may have been unnamed and to recognize its negativity, even if it was not realized at the time. More importantly, they are relevant to tracing the direct line that many find between Luther's teachings and extreme expressions of anti-Semitism in later centuries that are said to draw from Luther's teachings.

> It is shocking that Luther's ignoble name is still honored rather than forever cursed by mainstream Protestant churches. The continued honoring of Luther conveys a dangerous message, a message that was not lost on Hitler: namely, that a person's other accomplishments will earn him a position of respect in history, even if he has called for the destruction of world Jewry.[3]

The facts are less important than the attitude. Luther never called for the destruction of world Jewry. And perhaps the conflation of Luther's views with later historical realities to which he contributed is itself one of the knots that must be untied. But what is important in this quote is the recognition that Luther, seen from Jewish eyes, should not be honored, let alone considered a source of religious inspiration, in view of his negative and harmful attitude and recommendations toward the Jews and their historical realization in his time and continuing up to the Third Reich.[4]

Shortly before the above quote, Dershowitz lists the prac-

Anti-Semitism in the Age of Renaissance and Reformation (Philadelphia: Fortress Press, 1984), 102.

3. Alan M. Dershowitz, *Chutzpah* (New York: Simon & Schuster, 1991), 107. As Thomas Kaufmann notes, the line "from Luther to Hitler" has found acceptance among various English-speaking scholars. See Thomas Kaufmann, "Luther and the Jews," in *Jews, Judaism, and the Reformation in Sixteenth-Century Germany*, ed. Dean Phillip Bell and Stephen Burnett (Leiden: Brill, 2006), 103.

4. One notable instance of identification with Luther to justify acts committed during this period is offered by Julius Streicher, who defended himself as doing nothing more than following in the Reformer's footsteps. See Carter Lindberg, "Tainted Greatness: Luther's Attitudes toward Judaism and Their Historical Recep-

tical recommendations that appear at the end of *On the Jews and Their Lies*, Luther's essay on the Jews written in 1543. These recommendations include: burning, or completely razing, synagogues for the honor of Christ and Christendom; destroying Jews' homes; having all Jews' books, "prayer books, the Talmudic text and the whole Bible" taken from them; banning Jewish religious worship; suspending provisions for safe conduct for Jews; having all Jews' cash and treasures of gold and silver taken from them; expelling Jews from the country, "so let's get rid of them all."[5]

While this list does not include extermination of Jews, it is bad, certainly from a Jewish perspective, and by now one recognizes how problematic it is even from a universal perspective.

These recommendations come close to the end of a literary career that includes intensive engagement with the idea of Jews and Judaism. In the course of his career, especially near its end, Luther expressed himself negatively toward Judaism in ways that are extreme, even in the context of the Middle Ages. Luther's negativity is expressed in two tracks, a distinction necessary on substantive as well as on historical grounds. The one track involves accusations often leveled at Jews in the Middle Ages, including ritual murder, poisoning of wells, blasphemy against Christians, desecration of the host, and a variety of other stereotypical charges that were common at the time. Significantly, Luther's earlier works avoid these

tion," in *Tainted Greatness: Antisemitism and Cultural Heroes*, ed. Nancy A. Harrowitz (Philadelphia: Temple University Press, 1994), 15.

5. These recommendations are discussed in detail in chapter 5 of Thomas Kaufmann, *Luther's Jews: A Journey into Anti-Semitism* (Oxford: Oxford University Press, 2017). I have found this work to be the most helpful in understanding Luther in historical context and in offering a detailed presentation of the evolution of his views and attitudes in historical and biographical context. Kaufmann provides the references for these and the following paragraphs.

charges, during a phase in which Luther differed from common attitudes and espoused a positive treatment of Jews, arguing against their social and economic marginalization. The other track is theological. Here Luther is consistent throughout his career. Luther was an Old Testament professor, and the interpretation of Scripture was the core of his life. Luther read the Old Testament in light of the New Testament and was convinced that the christological reading of the Old Testament is the one and only valid reading of Scripture. This was at odds with Jewish readings. Luther did not allow for multiple interpretations or for the ongoing validity of the Jewish religion. The Talmud was false, the Jews were wrong, they had moved away from true religion, and they were obstinate, refusing to see truth. Ultimately, there was only one explanation for their obstinacy: their affiliation with the devil. Luther could not imagine any other explanation for why Jews would refuse to see the truth. Consistent throughout his career was the perception of Judaism's falsehood and of the stubbornness of the Jewish people in refusing to see the truth, represented in Christ, as key to the correct understanding of the Old Testament. The foundation for his negativity toward the Jews was theological and thus consistent throughout his career. What changed in the different periods was the approach and the scope of his negativity. The earlier Luther, especially around the publication of his 1523 work *That Jesus Christ was Born a Jew*, was more understanding, more loving, more inviting in practical ways, while the later Luther was hard and harsh. What also changed were the various nontheological accusations made. If in the earlier period Luther rejected these as false claims, in his later works he joined popular opinion in condemning the Jews for a host of harmful activities toward society and Christian religion.

In dealing with Luther, then, we deal with someone who was consistently opposed to Jews and Judaism. Despite the presence of antisemitic perspectives even in the early Luther, there is a significant divide between the early and the late Luther. The earlier Luther makes positive recommendations for the Jews, ascribing what is wrong with them to earlier Catholic policies towards them. The later Luther ascribes the wrongs to the Jews, not to other Christians.It might therefore be justified to distinguish between the earlier phase as anti-Judaism and the later phase as anti-semitism.[6] Regardless, Luther is bad news for the Jews and much theological will is required to identify a positive approach towards this enemy of the Jews.

Recognizing that medieval Christianity could not own Judaism as a full and valid religion, Luther offers in his person two models for Christian views and treatment of Jews and Judaism. He represents the best that medieval tradition can offer, as well as its worst. No other person contains such paradoxes in his person. And in this, Luther is iconic. As Heiko Oberman writes, "the terrible tragedy of the relationship between the Jews and Christians in world history can be studied in concentrated form in the history of this one man."[7] Perhaps it is not too much to add that in the same way that Luther represents the fullest of paradoxes and depth of tragedy, so too the prospect of finding new ways of appreciating him and of contextualizing his attitude to the Jews (and drawing lessons for our time from it) holds a key

6. Consider Eric Gritsch's discussion of Siegele-Wenschkewitz in Eric W. Gritsch, *Martin Luther's Anti-Semitism: Against His Better Judgment* (Grand Rapids: Eerdmans, 2012), 136. In what follows, I will refer to anti-Semitism as present in the early Luther as well, based on the work of Gritsch and Probst.

7. Heiko A. Oberman, *Luther: Man between God and Devil* (New York: Image, 1992), 296. See also Oberman, *Roots of Anti-Semitism*, 123; Betsy Halpern Amaru, "Martin Luther and Jewish Mirrors," *Jewish Social Studies* 46, no. 2 (1984): 101.

to advancing in how we deal with (or view) those troubled parts of the relationship that are represented in his person. This is how Rabbi Marc Tanenbaum saw it:

> The task for us in this irenic time, this age of pluralism and growing dialogue, is to try to approach the issue of Luther and his teachings with something of the same method by which many Christians and Jews today approach the cumbersomeness of their inherited tradition. Our task always is to separate out the essential teachings of the faith which are healing and redemptive, productive of love and mutual respect, and simply to repudiate that of the past which is no longer relevant or appropriate and was a historical response for another time.
>
> If papal infallibility is not in place, all the more so for Luther. If there's anything that should characterize the observance of the five hundredth birthday of Luther, I feel it should be the determination to face the bad in past tradition and to replace it by building a culture filled with caring, understanding and above all—knowledge of one another, not as caricatures and stereotypes, but as we are, committed Jews and Christians.[8]

It is important to begin our enquiry with the recognition of the problematic aspects of Luther. We must recognize these if we are to open a conversation that allows us to move beyond them. As Kaufmann states:

> Luther's hostility to the Jews was not simply the "shadow side" of his "inner self," his personality, or his theology, which we can underplay or obscure without making any fundamental difference to how he might be viewed as a whole, for a shadow cannot be separated from the body that casts it. Luther's anti-Semitism is an integral component of his personality and theology and can be viewed correctly only through a consistently historicizing lens. This is precisely what many people who feel "close" to Luther find particularly difficult. Seeing the reformer

8. Marc Tanenbaum, "Luther and the Jews: From the Past, a Present Challenge," in *A Prophet for Our Time: An Anthology of the Writings of Rabbi Marc H. Tanenbaum*, ed. Judith H. Banki and Eugene J. Fischer (New York: Fordham University Press, 2002), 275. Tanenbaum is referring to the five hundredth anniversary of Luther's birth.

> in historical context is the only option, however, and creates the right critical distance.[9]

Kaufmann here suggests one way of dealing with Luther's problematic legacy: recognizing it in its historical context. This is indeed one of the strategies that one can and must adopt. In what follows, I would like to offer three interrelated approaches to Luther's problematic legacy as a condition for and as part of a Jewish conversation on Luther. One is the view of Luther in his historical context. The second is an attempt to understand Luther from within, that is, from within his theological framework, religious coherence, and personal context and circumstances in relation to Jews. But before embarking on these two approaches, I would like to introduce a third dimension of our discussion. So far, we have only heard voices that are critical of Luther and that make his legacy problematic and not meaningful to a Jewish-Christian conversation. However, this is not how Luther has always been viewed by Jewish authors. There is a significant trajectory of appreciation of Luther by Jewish authors, extending past the Second World War. How do authors who belong to this trajectory deal with Luther's negative legacy? What do they find in him that makes him worthy of their appreciation and admiration? In what ways is their Luther a positive figure in Jewish eyes? Listening to these voices will provide a counterpoint to the critical voices we have heard.

9. Kaufmann, *Luther's Jews*, 156.

2.

The Jews and Luther

What is the history of Jewish views on Luther, and to what extent does this history justify the quest for giving Luther a positive hearing despite his negativity toward Jews and Judaism? Jewish views vary depending on the period and on how Luther's legacy is presented at any given point in time. The appearance of *That Jesus Christ Was Born a Jew* in 1523 was recognized as a watershed point in Christian views of Judaism.[1] This work advanced toleration of Jews more than any other work of the period.[2] This led to a positive appreciation of Luther in Jewish circles. Echoes of a novel approach to Jews spread throughout the Jewish world.[3] It was not only the call for toleration that was novel. It was also the tone, the empathy, and the recognition of religious commonality even

1. For a discussion of this work and the quotes below, see Thomas Kaufmann, *Luther's Jews: A Journey into Anti-Semitism* (Oxford: Oxford University Press, 2017), chapter 3.

2. Kaufmann, *Luther's Jews*, 4.

3. Hayim Hillel Ben-Sasson, "The Reformation in Contemporary Jewish Eyes," *Proceedings of the Israel Academy of Sciences and Humanities* 4 (Jerusalem: Israel Academy of Sciences and Humanities, 1970): 239–326.

within the framework of the exclusively Christian theological view that Luther espoused. Thus, Luther could write:

> For our fools the popes, bishops, sophists and monks, all stupid donkeys, have treated the Jews in such a way that anyone who was a good Christian would have been apt to become a Jew. And if I had been a Jew and had seen such idiots and thick-heads in charge of and teaching the Christian faith I would have rather become a pig than a Christian.[4]

One can see why Jews would have been happy hearing this. In its sixteenth-century context, this was novel, as revolutionary as many of the revolutions that Luther brought about within Christianity. Luther has practical recommendations that would spell improvement in the condition of the Jews. He asks,

> Forbidding them to work and trade or have any shared human existence with us, thus driving them to usury, how is that going to improve them?[5]

Accordingly, Luther recommends Jews be allowed to take up professions of their choice. Significantly, he appeals to the ideal of love.

> The law of Christian love [should be] practiced on them and they should be received kindly and allowed to trade and work with us, to live alongside us, and to hear and see our Christian teaching and way of life.[6]

While the deeper drive remains missionary, in practical terms there is a call for significant improvement of Jewish lives under the guiding principle of Christian love.

4. Martin Luther, *D. Martin Luthers Werke*, 127 vols. (Weimar: H. Böhlau, 1883–2009), 11:314–15 (series hereafter cited as WA), quoted in Kaufmann, *Luther's Jews*, 59.

5. WA 11:336, quoted in Kaufmann, *Luther's Jews*, 59.

6. WA 11:336, quoted in Kaufmann, *Luther's Jews*, 60.

Much of what is taken for granted nowadays in Jewish-Christian relations is articulated in this work as a novelty. Christians should deal with Jews as brothers. Jews are of the same blood as Jesus, an affirmation of a fundamental association of Jesus to Judaism. God has distinguished the Jewish people by calling the Savior, apostles, and prophets from amongst them. There is thus a sense of Jewish-Christian commonality and common ground, grounded in history and in the particularity of the life of the early church. It is perhaps worth noting that Luther does not speak of Jews and Christians having the Hebrew Bible (Old Testament) in common. For Luther, Christians possessed the fullness of revelation and the key to correct interpretation of the Bible in light of Christ, an interpretation the Jews refused. Thus, even though both communities appealed to the Bible, this was not considered by him as common ground. Luther was not in search of Jewish-Christian harmony or reparation. He was in search of convincing the Jews of the truth of Christianity. His toleration could therefore find expression on historical grounds, not by appeal to contemporary religious realities.

Even if this falls far below what would be acceptable to us today, it was novel and even revolutionary in Luther's day. And Jews responded accordingly, eliciting great admiration for the Reformer and relating these developments to Jewish messianic expectations.[7]

Luther's change of heart in relation to the Jews led to a similar change of attitude among contemporary leaders. A pun on the Hebrew transcription of Luther's name reads "the impure one."[8]

7. Pinchas Lapide, "Stimmen jüdischer Zeitgenossen zu Martin Luther," in *Die Juden und Martin Luther—Martin Luther und die Juden*, ed. H. Kremers (Neukirchen: Neukirchener, 1985), 171–88.

8. Nevertheless, in the latter part of the sixteenth century, Jewish historians took a

And yet, the response of Jews to the later Luther is not the final word on Jewish appreciation of Luther. For five hundred years, Jewish views of Luther oscillated between appreciation and admiration or condemnation and rejection. To no small extent, the pendulum swings according to which Luther one is relating to: the earlier or later Luther. From our historical vantage point, the later Luther dominates in view of the enormously harmful consequences of his recommendations once they were translated into German and Nazi racist policies toward Jews. But for hundreds of years, both Protestants and Jews could think of Luther while ignoring his later recommendations. The history of Luther's reception is one of selective acceptance of his teachings.[9] If some Lutherans only integrated the younger Luther into their view of the Jews (and for extended periods this was the norm), Jews would have felt at ease with Luther and his heirs. This is reflected in a lengthy trajectory of Jewish appreciation of Luther. Significantly, this trajectory takes place in a German context, where Luther is a founding cultural figure and a central figure to whom one appeals as part of the Jewish quest for being integrated into German society and culture. Consequently, most if not all the following expressions of admiration for Luther come out of movements that seek absorption into the broader

broader view, seeing the Reformation as the fulfillment of age-old dreams and ignoring the suffering caused by the later Luther. See Abraham David, "The Lutheran Reformation in Sixteenth-Century Jewish Historiography," *Jewish Studies Quarterly* 10, no. 2 (2003): 139.

9. This is detailed in chapter 6 of Kaufmann, *Luther's Jews*. See also Johannes Wallmann, "The Reception of Luther's Writings on the Jews from the Reformation to the End of the 19th Century," in *Stepping-Stones to Further Jewish-Lutheran Relationships*, ed. Harold H. Ditmanson (Minneapolis: Augsburg, 1990), 120–44. Gritsch, *Martin Luther's Anti-Semitism*, chapter 3, offers a historical survey of Luther's reception. Gritsch's review lends significance to the distinction between the early and the late Luther, inasmuch as, in his reading, the later Luther was not able to undo the positive impressions of the early Luther, as measured by the reception history of his work (Gritsch, *Martin Luther's Anti-Semitism*, 158–59). See further Lindberg, "Tainted Greatness," 22–26.

culture and that are associated with Jewish reform. It would make sense for Jewish reformers to identify themselves with or to feel close to "The Reformer."[10] Let us hear some relevant voices. Thus, Solomon Ludwig Steinheim (1789–1866):

> Let us honour the hero of the sixteenth century, the great, marvellous German, who unfurled the banner of freedom of thought in the highest and purest region of human thought, the thought of and about God, from the spiritual bondage of the Inquisition with his strong arms, and raised it in honour of humanity, once more high on the standpoint of the spirit! Blessed be the memory of Luther, in spite of all that he may have erred in word and deed! Let his memory be holy to us also![11]

Reference to a holy memory is probably as high an honor as one could imagine. The quote is interesting in that it does not suggest perfection. It recognizes Luther's errors "in word and deed," a likely, though not absolutely necessary, reference to Luther's views toward the Jews. If so, we find willingness to recognize his greatness and to own his memory as holy, even while acknowledging his wrongdoings toward the Jews. In similar vein, the great Jewish philosopher Hermann Cohen applies to Luther fully the Jewish formula "Martin Luther of blessed memory."[12] Cohen says nothing of the anti-Semitic Luther. To cope with the contradiction in the

10. Sources for what follows are taken from Christian Wiese, "'Let His Memory Be Holy to Us': Jewish Interpretations of Martin Luther from the Enlightenment to the Holocaust," *Leo Baeck Institute Yearbook* 54 (2009): 93–126. See further Dorothea Wendebourg, "'Gesegnet sei das Andenken Luthers!': Die Juden und Martin Luther im 19. Jahrhundert," *Zeitschrift fur Religions und Geistesgeschichte* 65, no. 3 (2013): 235–51. While she covers much of the same ground, it is interesting to note Wendebourg's study of Jewish contributions to Jubilees celebrating Luther. The present work is accordingly in line with a long-standing "tradition."

11. Salomon Ludwig Steinheim, *Die Offenbarung nach dem Lehrbegriffe der Synagoge*, vol. 3 (Leipzig: Oskar Leiner, 1863), 246, quoted in Wiese, "Let His Memory," 110–11.

12. Wiese, "Let His Memory," 118.

historical Luther, Cohen claims that the historical Luther is not the most important thing; rather, it is the idea of Reformation.

It is most interesting to note how Franz Rosenzweig refers to Luther. Rosenzweig refers to him as a religious genius.[13]

As Christian Wiese argues, Jews appealed to Luther as a way of countering the inhuman logic of modern anti-Semitism. The attempt was ultimately both an illusionary apologetic strategy and an act of intellectual resistance that deserves the historian's respect. Considered retrospectively, the Jewish affair with Luther would seem a tragic illusion, with Jewish authors blind to the reality of the Reformer's true views and the lack of contemporary Protestantism's response to their dialogical approach.[14]

In some ways, we are better off today than were these German-Jewish voices in thinking of Luther. If each generation had its own Luther, today's Luther, the post-World War II Luther, could no longer be presented independently of his anti-Semitic face. This means that both Jews and Christians are challenged to confront Luther in a more real way, somehow accommodating Luther's shadow side even as they seek to appreciate his greatness, his genius. It is therefore interesting to consider some rabbinic voices (again: reform), that seek to come to terms with Luther following the holocaust. Pinchas Lapide's presentation of Luther recognizes the distinction between the earlier and the later Luther. Against

13. As I show in chapter 10 of *Religious Genius*, the term enjoyed some currency in the early part of the twentieth century and then largely fell into disuse. Rosenzweig's use thus reflects this earlier phase of appeal to the term. This is not the only such usage I have come across. Albert Friedlander, cited below, refers to Luther as genius toward the close of the twentieth century. Other applications of the term are found. Ernst Troeltsch referred to Luther using the same term as Rosenzweig, almost at the same time. See Wiese, "Let His Memory," 115n100.

14. Wiese, "Let His Memory," 126.

such recognition, his application of Jeremiah 2:2: "I remember the *chesed* [love, grace] of your youth" rings with particular poignancy.[15]

By far the most moving and inspiring Jewish view of Luther is offered by Rabbi Albert Friedlander.[16] Friedlander begins by citing Karl Jaspers's identification of Luther's writings as the source of Nazism. Yet, he insists, this cannot prevent Jews from recognizing Luther's greatness. Significantly, Friedlander too refers to Luther in terms of genius. The power of Friedlander's presentation owes, in part, to his being able to relate to the later Luther's recommendations against the Jews from his personal and family experience in Berlin of the 1930s.

In confronting the challenge of how to deal with the imperfection attached to Luther's greatness, he appeals to rabbinic anthropology. For the rabbis, every person has two inclinations, a good one and an evil one. The later Luther simply gave in or was overpowered by his evil inclination.[17] Friedlander is willing to allow genius and moral imperfection to coexist in a person. In fact, the coexistence of spirit and chaos in a person is itself the secret of genius.

Friedlander is willing to insert himself into a dialogue with Luther, rather than simply reject him or dismiss him as a false teacher based on personal experience during the Third Reich. He is willing to ask questions such as "What would Luther want of me?"—questions that are typically reserved for the commanding voice of traditional religious authorities. Similarly, he is willing to insert himself into a personal

15. Lapide, "Stimmen jüdischer Zeitgenossen zu Martin Luther," 183.

16. Albert Friedlander, "Martin Luther und wir Juden," in *Die Juden und Martin Luther—Martin Luther und die Juden*, ed. H. Kremers (Neukirchen: Neukirchener, 1985), 289–300.

17. Friedlander, "Martin Luther und wir Juden," 290.

dialogue with Luther. His rhetoric strategy for dealing with the chronology of early and late is to change the frame of reference from temporal to spatial. Early and late are replaced by the metaphor of different chambers in Luther's house. The higher chambers contain the library, where Luther and he can share in the reading and interpretation of Scripture. Friedlander introduces an important topos in Jewish-Christian relations that, as suggested above, is actually absent from Luther himself: commonality of Scripture.[18] For Friedlander, Luther's work as a translator and his need to also consult Jewish knowledge on the meaning of words makes the Bible a common meeting ground.[19] In the course of such a meeting, the two exist face to face. Friedlander would be seen by Luther.[20] That Luther can affirm Jesus as a Jew creates a common ground that would allow for compassion and deeper human sharing.

However, the later Luther occupies the dungeon, a dark part of the house where there are no windows, where there

18. As Salo Baron has noted, Luther's lifetime preoccupation with the Old Testament made him, on the whole, less, rather than more, friendly to contemporary Jews. See Salo Wittmayer Baron, *A Social and Religious History of the Jews*, vol. 13, *Inquisition, Renaissance, and Reformation* (New York: Columbia University Press, 1969), 220. The argument for Jewish-Christian commonality based on sharing of Scriptures can be dated to a Jewish contemporary of Luther's, Josel of Rosheim. See Debra Kaplan, "Sharing Conversations: A Jewish Polemic against Martin Luther," *Archiv fur Reformationsgeschichte* 103, no. 1 (2012): 62.

19. Actually, Luther had a very negative view of Christian Hebraism and consulting Jewish readings of Scripture. See Kaufmann, *Luther's Jews*, 101ff. Luther would not have recognized this later historical trope as part of his own relationship with Jews.

20. There is scholarly consensus that this is the opposite of how Luther would have seen the matter. He would neither recognize the Jews as legitimate bearers of scriptural truth and interpretation, nor be able to see them for what they are. Betsy Halpern Amaru has captured this very well in her reference to Luther as viewing Jews in mirrors. Throughout, Luther projects his views and imaginations on Jews rather than encountering them as real individuals. See Betsy Halpern Amaru, "Martin Luther and Jewish Mirrors," *Jewish Social Studies* 46, no. 2 (1984): 95–102. Friedlander retrojects a latter-day evolution of Jewish-Christian relations back upon Luther.

is no light, and where Friedlander, the Jew, is not seen by Luther. While he exists, he is not seen. Friedlander thus points to a central cause of Luther's attitude to Jews: lack of proper, firsthand knowledge of Jews.[21] The spatial metaphor allows Friedlander to issue an invitation to Luther suggesting it is time they get back to the higher levels of the house, where commonality and mutual visibility are possible.

Friedlander's is the most powerful and evocative, even inspiring, Jewish voice reflecting on Luther. The historical foundations of his reconstruction are less significant than the willingness of a learned scholar, familiar with current literature on Luther and the Jews, to recognize, accept, and legitimate Luther and to issue an invitation for coming together again as in the higher levels of the mansion. The negativity that issued from Luther cannot take away from the light and understanding that are still made possible with reference to Luther.

21. Historically, this is as true of the earlier Luther as it is of the later. See Kaufmann, *Luther's Jews*, chapter 1. Friedlander relies on Luther's work as translator of the Bible as an effective substitute for proper relations with Jews.

3.

Luther in Historical Context

"Seeing the Reformer in historical context is the only option, however, and creates the right critical distance." Thus Kaufmann, quoted above. There are various aspects to what might be meant by "historical context." The transition of early to late Luther has its own historical context, to be explored below. For the present moment, I would like to concentrate upon Luther's anti-Semitism in historical context. It is difficult to appreciate the Reformer's recommendations on Judaism, either the early ones or the late ones, without having a sense of what the historical reality was prior to Luther's activity. Several scholars have devoted studies to this question.[1]

There seems to be consensus on the matter, a consensus

1. In addition to relevant discussions in Thomas Kaufmann, *Luther's Jews: A Journey into Anti-Semitism* (Oxford: Oxford University Press, 2017), these include Jeremy Cohen, "Traditional Prejudice and Religious Reform: The Theological and Historical Foundations of Luther's Anti-Judaism," in *Anti-Semitism in Times of Crisis*, ed. Sander L. Gilman and Steven T. Katz (New York: New York University Press, 1991), 81–102; Marc Tanenbaum, "Luther and the Jews: From the Past, a Present Challenge," in *A Prophet for Our Time: An Anthology of the Writings of Rabbi Marc H. Tanenbaum*, ed. Judith H. Banki and Eugene J. Fischer (New York: Fordham University Press, 2002). These studies reference additional ones.

articulated by the Luther scholar Ernest Gordon Rupp. The appropriate way of dealing with "Luther's Jews" was to see them in historical context, by locating the Reformer in the history of medieval anti-Semitism. In this history, Luther was, says Rupp, an appalling, disgraceful chapter, but no more than one chapter.[2] Jeremy Cohen has studied Luther in comparative historical context by focusing on three points: understanding the relationship of the old and new covenants, the propriety of engagement of Christian scholars in Jewish studies, and the revulsion with which Luther reacted to contemporary Jews and Judaism. A study of these areas, some across almost fifteen centuries, leads Cohen to conclude that Luther was not more anti-Semitic than his broader environment or his close historical predecessors. As Tanenbaum remarks, the tradition of demonizing the Jews—a tradition that Luther became a spokesperson for, grounding and incorporating it in his hermeneutical and theological oeuvre—has existed since the first century.[3] For this reason, dealing with Luther is dealing not simply with Luther but with an entire aspect of Jewish-Christian relations. Seen against the background of his contemporaries, "what distinguished Luther's position from that of his contemporaries . . . was the exorbitant ferocity of his polemic and the dramatic change that occurred in his standpoint on how the Jews should be treated."[4]

Let us spell out the implications of this recognition for both the young and the old Luther. Beginning with the latter, Luther's views and recommendations in relation to the Jews are not novel or radical seen against his historical context. The negative view of Jews and their association with the devil

2. Kaufmann, *Luther's Jews*, 151.
3. Tanenbaum, "Luther and the Jews," 265.
4. Kaufmann, *Luther's Jews*, 153.

has a long pedigree. Various negative descriptions of Jews who poison wells, kill children, and so forth were common in Luther's time and society. We are justified in asking what made Luther identify with these descriptions, especially having renounced them consciously in his earlier writings. But what he resorts to are stock motives, common in his environment.

The same is true of his recommendations, some of which were harmful to Jews in the immediate future and some of which matured into poisonous positions several centuries later. These recommendations were not new. They had been practiced, and some of them were even the norm. Let us consider expulsion of the Jews. The issue of permission for Jews to settle in particular localities was an ongoing feature of the interaction of Jews with Christian society and an indication of the precarity of their situation. As a consequence of the application of this policy, Luther barely had contact with Jews. They had been expelled. That the older Luther reached, on psychological or theological grounds, the conclusion that Jews had to be separated from Christians was no more than the application of an existing historical solution to the problems that confronted him. Significantly, he never considered mass murder of Jews. His solution was to have them live in Turkish lands, with other people who lack faith, to avoid contaminating the purity of Christian society. The various measures he recommends can similarly be analyzed against historical precedents. Luther's authority made his recommendations more potent and harmful than had they been voiced by another or simply been the carry-over of an earlier age. But in this, Luther was not an innovator.

It was actually the earlier Luther who was the innovator. The recommendations to treat the Jews with Christian love, to allow them to become members of society, and to reach out to them in a kind and loving way, in the course of missionary outreach, were new. Luther could formulate them in part because it was convenient for him to identify the present condition of the Jews with the Catholics who were to blame for the state of the Jews. But it is likely that Luther's attitude toward the Jews was more than using them as pawns in his battle against Rome. Let us consider that a spirit of benevolence, a spiritual vision, something of a more "enlightened" approach, characterizes the early Luther in relation to the Jews. As noted above, Jews certainly perceived it in this way. Where did this new approach come from? We may be justified in recognizing here Luther's own spirit, his greatness, perhaps even his genius, in offering a loving and humane solution at a time when many others were neither able to act nor to think in this way.[5]

When Jewish authors who admired Luther gravitated to the early Luther, it is not only because these works offered a positive approach to the Jews, contrasted with his later writings. It is also because a certain spirit manifests in these writings, especially against the background of the times, through which Luther's greatness emerged.[6]

Once things are framed in this way, we need to consider what it was that led to Luther's change of heart. More broadly: what were the factors that led to Luther's negative view of the Jews? Can we understand how he came to hold

5. Luther was by no means the only one to think of the Jews in positive terms. For a presentation of other Reformers' views on Jews, see Eric W. Gritsch, *Martin Luther's Anti-Semitism: Against His Better Judgment* (Grand Rapids: Eerdmans, 2012), 26; Christian M. Rutishauser, "500 Jahre Reformation, 50 Jahre Reformkonzil—und das Judentum," *Stimmen der Zeit*, no. 1, 2017, 6.

6. This would be relevant for later generations. Jews probably did not actually read Luther, as opposed to hearing of his teachings, until the nineteenth century. See Debra Kaplan, "Sharing Conversations: A Jewish Polemic against Martin Luther," *Archiv fur Reformationsgeschichte* 103, no. 1 (2012): 62.

the views he held and why he adopted his later views? That certain views were current in his environment and have a venerable anti-Semitic pedigree does not yet account for why Luther adopted these positions. As we have seen, he not only could, he did in fact hold the opposite positions in his earlier years. A historical view of Luther must therefore seek to account for why Luther held the negative beliefs he did toward the Jews.

Understanding Luther's reasons should not lead to exonerating him of the charges of anti-Semitism, let alone to justifying his views. I enter into this territory, which has been adequately covered by the extensive literature on the subject, for two reasons. The first is that if we can answer "what went wrong" in ways other than saying that he succumbed to conventional beliefs and opinions, we may learn fundamental dynamics about relations between faith communities, a view of the religious other, and the particularities of what can go wrong in Jewish-Christian relations. If we can identify where things go wrong, contained therein is the promise of reparation and healing. Moreover, without attempting to detract from the burden on the later Luther's conscience, one may project, based on our knowledge of human relationships and intergroup relations, that when things go wrong, they rarely go wrong in a unidirectional way. In close relationships—and a hate relationship can also be a close one—dynamics may be replicated and find parallel expressions across the divide that distinguishes two parties. Therefore, if we can get past condemning Luther and seek to identify the deeper dynamics that led to his adoption of radical stances in relation to Judaism in his teaching and addresses, we may enter a domain that both Jews and Christians need to visit. Without seeking to create equivalence or to relativize the horrendous consequences of theologically based anti-Semitism, we may consider whether any of the relational, attitudinal, and social dimensions that help us make sense of Luther and the evolution of his thought might have lessons that apply to Jews. If Luther is revisited from the perspective of contemporary Jewish-Christian relations, this must mean more than Christians apologizing and repenting for Luther's anti-Semitism. A serious study of any formative relationship, let alone one as complex as that of Luther toward the Jews, is bound to deliver lessons for both parties. In fact, as will be suggested, the lessons are broad and should address relations of diverse faith traditions as they view themselves and one another. In the same way that the Jews were not the sole recipients of Luther's venom, so the lessons from considering "what went wrong," or what led to Luther's positions, apply not only to Jews and Christians but potentially to all.

4.

Introducing the "Luther Model"

Much has been written on Luther and Judaism, and the personal, historical, and theological circumstances that informed the evolution of Luther's thought and, in particular, his later writings. In what follows, I will present the various dimensions that informed Luther's attitudes in categories and key points, allowing us a synthetic view of the factors that impacted Luther's consciousness and views. These I will refer to as "the Luther model." It is by means of this model that Luther can be made to speak to the broader issue of religion going wrong, and to thereby serve as a teacher not only for Christians but also for Jews—victims of Luther's anti-Semitism—as well as to people of other religions. Let us then review the various dimensions that make up "the Luther model."

1. LACK OF CONTACT WITH JEWS AND NO MEANINGFUL FIRSTHAND KNOWLEDGE OF JEWS

Luther had almost no contact with Jews. While the Jews occupy a very central position in his theology, he had, in fact, very little contact with real Jews. The entire issue of "Luther and the Jews" has to be understood in literary, theoretical, theological, and imaginary terms, but almost not at all in terms of real contact with Jews. There were no Jews in Wittenberg in Luther's time. They had been expelled. Of the various places associated with Luther's biography, there was a small Jewish community in Eisleben. One of the last communications by Luther, days before his death, attributes his having gotten sick to the presence of the Jews in town.[1] It was not the Jews as real personalities but rather their imagined presence, a feared enemy, a negative force, that impacted Luther's imagination down to his dying days. Betsy Halpern Amaru has referred to how Luther projects on Jews as "Jewish mirrors." She helpfully suggests that both the early Luther and the late Luther are expressions of such "mirrors," reflections of Luther's imagination and understanding. Both capture different aspects of how the Jews are perceived, by Luther and by broader society. However, they have little to do with the Jews themselves and certainly do not grow out of real encounters with Jews.

We know of several incidents of exchanges between Luther and Jews.[2] These include a friendly relationship with Josel of Rosheim, representative of the Jewish communities to the emperor's court. However, for the most part, Luther's

1. See Thomas Kaufmann, *Luther's Jews: A Journey into Anti-Semitism* (Oxford: Oxford University Press, 2017), 2–3.

2. These are surveyed in Kaufmann, *Luther's Jews*.

exchanges with Jews hinged on Jewish-Christian debates. It matters little if it was Jews who came to see him having heard of his Reformation or Jews he encountered under other circumstances. What stands at the heart of these exchanges is the status of Jews in relation to Christians. Conversion, and again it matters little whether it is from Judaism to Christianity or the reverse, looms large. What we lack are normal day-to-day relations of people who live together and share a common existence. Jews were not part of Luther's real world, even if we can recount a handful of events relating to encounters.

To understand just how little Jews were part of his world, we must realize that, in fact, Jews were in some way beyond society itself. Having been banished from most areas where Luther lived, their existence was a kind of shadow existence. It is reminiscent of the existence of Roma communities today, occasionally seen, always other, typically menacing, a source of worry and concern, not subject of common friendly exchange.

In many ways, this fact provides the foundation for the various other issues that dog Luther's relations with Jews. For most of Christian history, Jews and Christians lived together and had relationships, even if those were fraught with difficulties and challenges. The extreme negativity shown by Luther toward Jews is almost unparalleled in the history of Jewish-Christian relations and it is even more perplexing given the change in Luther's attitude. It is only against the backdrop of lack of personal knowledge and personal relationships that we can bring together the different factors that combined to make up Luther's attitudes to the Jews. Had he had Jewish friends, it is likely that his entire view would have been different.[3]

3. Johannes Wallmann ("Luther on Jews and Islam," in *Creative Biblical Exegesis:*

2. WRONG AND MISLEADING KNOWLEDGE AND INFORMATION

One should relate the lack of friends to the lack of Jewish teachers and informants. The time of the Reformation is closely related to the rise of Christian Hebraism and the interest that Christian scholars showed in learning from Jews. Luther opposed such efforts.[4] This opposition may be theologically based, but it had the net effect of further limiting Luther's direct contact with Jews. If learning from Jews creates some personal bonds and is based on a measure of trust, such internal posturing would be absent from the Reformer's life, given his objection to Christians learning from Jews.

If Luther had no Jewish friends, did not live in some closeness or proximity to Jews, and did not share in the turn to Jewish learning that characterized the efforts of some of his contemporaries, where did he get his knowledge of Jews and Judaism from? Luther's knowledge was a mix of popular lore and information that he received on specifically Jewish issues by "authorities" of the time. Popular lore was, on the whole, negative and was part of the problematic legacy of the Middle Ages that contributed to anti-Jewish feelings. Even more worrisome are Luther's authorities. His knowledge of Jews and their customs came from the works of converted Jews, especially Antonius Margaritha. It has been shown that Margaritha's work had a strong impact on Luther. One of Luther's works, on the Shem Hamephorash (how Jews apply the divine name), owes directly to information received from Margaritha. Luther may have considered himself on firm

Christian and Jewish Hermeneutics through the Centuries, JSOTSup 59 [Sheffield: JSOT Press, 1988], 151) presents the few points of contact as teaching us of ongoing relations between Luther and Jews. This is at odds with broader scholarly consensus.

4. See Kaufmann, *Luther's Jews*, 101ff., 124.

ground in relying on a presentation of Judaism by a former member of the Jewish community. However, in fact, Margaritha's work is highly biased and negative, in the manner often associated with Jewish converts to Christianity.

A second important source of "knowledge" on Judaism was the learned Sebastian Munster, whose anti-Judaism was as pronounced as Luther's. "The expert knowledge of two of his contemporaries, the learned convert Margaritha and the recognized hebraist Munster, confirmed for the reformer and biblical theologian Luther what he 'knew' from the witness of Church history and from the Bible, namely that the doctrine and life of the Jews was marked by hatred of Christ."[5] The theology professor may have been satisfied with the "academic" foundations provided by the sources he relied on. Clearly, we, and even many of his contemporaries, would have been able to discern the bias and negativity that had a very negative impact upon Luther's views of the Jews.

3. PERSONAL HURT AND OFFENSE AS A CONSEQUENCE OF DEEP RELIGIOUS ENGAGEMENT

Knowledge is shaped by how we receive it, how it touches us, and the emotional associations it evokes in us. This is all the more so in cases of conflict between religious communities or traditions and how the "knowledge" that serves such conflict impacts individuals. No one can take Luther's piety, deep faith, and devotion from him. While one rarely considers the personal religious depth in the same breath

5. Thomas Kaufmann, "Luther and the Jews," in *Jews, Judaism, and the Reformation in Sixteenth-Century Germany*, ed. Dean Phillip Bell and Stephen Burnett (Leiden: Brill, 2006), 94. See further Kaufmann, *Luther's Jews*, 109.

as viewing the anti-Semitic Luther, in fact there is a point of deep connection between them. The depth of piety and the emotion it conditioned in Luther were responsible for the intensity of his anti-Jewish feelings. Through the depth of piety, the "knowledge" and "information" he possessed concerning Jewish practices fed into historical processes.

One of the formative experiences of Luther was a report of an encounter with a Jew who refers to Jesus as the "hanged one" in accordance with a certain Jewish practice of avoiding Jesus's name or speaking of him in a noncomplimentary way. In terms of nuance and music, there is a significant distinction between "the hanged one" and "the crucified," though both seemingly describe the same reality.[6] Luther was deeply offended by this language, and in Kaufmann's description this amounts to a constitutive moment that defined Luther's relationship with Jews.[7] This formative moment receives strengthening from additional information concerning Jewish attitudes to Jesus. Luther learned of the *Toledot Yeshu* tradition, a negative Jewish portrayal of Jesus, a counternarrative to the gospel.[8] He also came to believe that Jews curse Jesus in the synagogue. If we cast aside for a moment the question of how reliable or representative the following report is, and only consider it from the perspective of Luther's emotions and subjective experience, as someone who is on the receiving end of what is described below, this will provide us with an important dimension for appreciating what fuels his animosity toward Jews.

> They wish us every kind of harm with curses, slanders and spitting beyond imagining. They wish that violence and wars,

6. For the negative biblical connotations of a dead man hanging, see Deut 21:23.
7. See Kaufmann, *Luther's Jews*, 30–35.
8. Kaufmann, *Luther's Jews*, 119.

> terror and every type of misery should overtake us accursed Goyim. They do this cursing every Saturday openly in their synagogues and daily in their own homes. They teach, encourage and accustom their children to do these things from their childhood onwards so that they will remain bitter, virulent and vicious enemies of Christians.[9]

This passage from *On the Jews and Their Lies* provides the emotional tone that fed Luther's vitriol.

4. PERSONAL TRAUMA AND PERSONAL FEARS

Luther's subjective experience was not limited to hurt. Another important dimension is fear. Fear is present in the overall attitude to Jews in Luther's time. The reference above to Jews causing what ended up being his final illness was not the whim of an anti-Semite. It was part of common mentality. If Jews are in the margins of society and beyond the boundaries of conventional community, then it is easy to associate various plagues, illnesses, and calamities with them. Luther shared in this broader orientation.

But Luther also had his own fears. One significant incident led Luther to believe that Jews were attempting to poison him.[10] Jewish doctors were on the whole seen by him as practicing poisoning of Christians. Once he believed this, it was only a small step to consider that there was actually a Jewish attempt on his life. From around 1525, Luther lived in existential fear of Jewish murderers, thinking they were out to poison him.[11] That the "poisoning Jew" did so in the service

9. Kaufmann, *Luther's Jews*, 113. On Jewish curses against Christians in Germano-Franco Judaism and on their impression on the Christians, see Israel Jacob Yuval, *Two Nations in Your Womb: Perceptions of Jews and Christians in Late Antiquity and the Middle Ages* (Berkeley: University of California Press, 2006), 130–34.

10. See Kaufmann, *Luther's Jews*, 37.

11. Kaufmann, *Luther's Jews*, 37.

of Catholics did not detract from the power of this "incident" to instill fear of Jews as an ongoing feature of Luther's emotional attitude toward the Jews.

5. THEOLOGICAL AND SCRIPTURAL FOUNDATIONS

Against the background of Luther the man, his psychology and personal orientation, we can now consider Luther the theologian. The theologian offers the theoretical foundations that not only solidify the negativity that is assumed and integrated through personal experience, but also make it incontestable, beyond the realm of dialogue and reason. For many readers of Luther, here is the heart of Luther's anti-Jewish feelings and eventually also his anti-Semitic attitudes.[12] Let us consider several basic facts that converge in the person of Luther, leading to such principled anti-Jewish attitudes.

Luther was a Bible professor and exegete. He spent the greater part of his career commenting on the Old Testament. Luther's reading assumes a unity of Old and New Testaments' and the method of such unity, in continuity with the earlier church, was to interpret the Old in light of the New. Consequently, his interpretation of the Old Testament was christological. Christ is the true subject of the Old Testament, and a correct reading of the Old Testament will point to him. Luther assumes one and only one possible reading of the Old Testament. He had no room in his interpretive economy for multiple interpretations. What that means, then, is that he had no room for Jews and their interpretation. Jew-

12. This is described effectively in Brooks Schramm, "Introduction: Martin Luther, the Bible and the Jewish People," in *Martin Luther, the Bible, and the Jewish People: A Reader*, ed. Brooks Schramm and Kirsi I. Stjerna (Minneapolis: Fortress Press, 2012), 3–20.

ish interpretation is belied by the message of the New Testament. Even if the early Luther had compassion for Jews, he had no patience for Judaism. At no point did he recognize in Judaism a legitimate expression of biblical interpretation.[13] Judaism was error, and in his world there was no room for religious pluralism.[14] From a theological perspective, which is the conscious engine of his teaching and communication, the Jews are those who refuse to heed the message of Scripture, hanging on to other, false readings of the shared Scripture. For Luther, unlike how Rabbi Friedlander would wish to see it, common Scripture is not a basis for commonality. It is, rather, a source of contention and argument. Jews refuse to see the true meaning of Scripture and prefer their false traditions instead. For Luther, Jewish refusal to recognize the true, christological meaning of Scripture was beyond comprehension. He was so convinced by his own method of reading that he could not imagine why Jews would refuse it. The existence of a community of interpreters who had owned the Scripture in the first instance and who continued to relate to it in a manner that defied Luther's own reading was a thorn in his side. From the intellectual and theological perspective, herein lies the source of Luther's opposition to Jews.

The attempt to account for why and how Jews would be so obstinate ultimately leads to the "unavoidable" conclusion that Jews are in alliance with the devil. The demonization of Jews was already a trope in the Middle Ages. One aspect of Luther's use of it was to solve a theological/historical crux that one imagines tortured him. For a principled thinker who cares for truth and for correct interpretation, refusal to share

13. Kaufmann, "Luther and the Jews," 97.

14. Eric W. Gritsch, "Luther and the Jews: Toward a Judgment of History," in *Stepping-Stones to Further Jewish-Lutheran Relationships*, ed. Harold H. Ditmanson (Minneapolis: Augsburg, 1990), 111.

in this truth is ultimately a metaphysical worry that can only be understood by appeal to some metaphysical reality, such as association with the devil.

From this perspective, one should not distinguish the young and the old Luther. The theological, and missiological, drive is consistent throughout.[15] The differences as to what measures should be applied to Jews as individuals do not change the theological foundations of Luther's approach to Jews. If there is no legitimacy for Judaism, conversion remains the only possible religious option.

Luther could have perhaps had a theological argument with Jews, and it could have been left at that, without taking center stage in his thought. However, Jews loom large in his thought, in part due to the place of Jews in the competition of interpretations. No less important is the strictly theological dimension. Luther's work amplifies dichotomies that are present in Paul, and these dichotomies in turn made the Jews ever present in his thinking. The centrality of justification, arguably a cornerstone in his theological edifice, led him to pit Christians (true Christians, who would follow his teaching over and against Catholics) against Jews and others (including Catholics). Jews became an expression of false religion. So much so that they were needed as illustrations of such false religion, thereby further reinforcing the problematic image of the Jew on theological grounds.

The entire edifice of Luther's theology in some way or another points to the antithesis of Judaism. Thus, notions like faith, salvation, grace, freedom, and Law and Gospel, all cen-

15. Ingemar Öberg, *Luther and World Mission: A Historical and Systematic Study* (St. Louis: Concordia, 2007), 328; Schramm, "Introduction: Martin Luther," 3; Gritsch, "Luther and the Jews," 113.

tral to his teaching, become intertwined with the dichotomy of Jew and Christian.[16]

The centrality of Jews to Luther's theological construction has led to contemporary reflections on where the problem with Luther's attitude to the Jews lies.[17] If Luther's practical recommendations against Jews and his anti-Semitism were simply part of medieval attitudes, they might have been bracketed. Similarly, if they were just the expressions of his psychological reactions, described above, or the consequences of his old age and its frailties, as some have suggested,[18] one could have done away with those portions of his heritage and concentrated on others. However, the deep penetration of Jews and Judaism within the theological fabric of his thinking leads to the question of whether the entire structure of his thought is flawed. How can one maintain some of the fundamental tensions and dichotomies of his thought while detaching them from their association with Jews and Judaism? This is one of the contemporary challenges of Lutheran thinkers.

Because of how deeply Luther engaged the theme of the Jews, and because of the theological roots of his negativity toward them, Luther was led to polemicizing against the Jews on theological grounds. One important motive in this polemic is the condition of the Jews. In the argument of interpretations, Luther appealed to Jewish history and to the present condition of the Jews as proof for the invalidity of Jewish interpretation. What validates interpretation is God,

16. Schramm, "Introduction: Martin Luther," 4.

17. Carter Lindberg, "Tainted Greatness: Luther's Attitudes toward Judaism and Their Historical Reception," in *Tainted Greatness: Antisemitism and Cultural Heroes*, ed. Nancy A. Harrowitz (Philadelphia: Temple University Press, 1994), 27; Christian M. Rutishauser, "500 Jahre Reformation, 50 Jahre Reformkonzil—und das Judentum," *Stimmen der Zeit*, no. 1, 2017, 6.

18. Lindberg, "Tainted Greatness," 18–19. See also sources brought by Heiko A. Oberman, *The Roots of Anti-Semitism in the Age of Renaissance and Reformation* (Philadelphia: Fortress Press, 1984), 128n27.

and Jewish history shows that God has abandoned the Jews. Luther could not conceive of any other explanation for 1,500 years of exile and the almost subhuman conditions of Jewish life. What for Jews is the highest sign of faith was not recognized by this theologian and was rather taken as a sign of rejection and invalidation of Jewish religion and scriptural interpretation.

Several contemporary scholars and thinkers comment on Luther's theological consistency and the consequences it leads to with reference to the Jews, in light of Luther's own principles of theologizing. Luther upheld a theology of the cross, not of glory. He taught an unknown God who transcends our understanding. And yet, when it came to the Jews, Luther's theology became one of glory, and Luther was able to interpret, prove, and justify from the witness of history, in accordance with his own theological scheme.[19] Contemporary scholars have referred to this as theological failure of nerve.[20] Differently expressed, this was done against his own better judgment.[21]

What is the drive that would lead to something that could be seen as a failure when judged within the theological system? I can see two factors at work. The first has to do with the urge for theological consistency. While one may not know the obscurities and the depth of divine will, Scripture does provide a key for interpretation of reality. It would seem that for Luther, his own scriptural reading and the certitude that it allowed him with reference to the Jews was such that he did not feel he was violating his own principles. Add to this the second factor, the need to simultaneously polemicize against the Jews and to make sense of a unique and inexplicable his-

19. Gritsch, *Martin Luther's Anti-Semitism*, 74–77.
20. Lindberg, "Tainted Greatness," 26.
21. Gritsch, *Martin Luther's Anti-Semitism*, 77, 96.

tory, and one can see how Luther would have been led to his conclusions. For us Jews and Christians who reflect on Judaism from a post-Holocaust perspective and from the perspective of a transformed history of redemptive return home, a different vantage point presents itself for viewing Jews and their faith, and consequently Luther and his theological failure of nerve. Yet, we must also appreciate the consistency, coherence, and logic of Luther's positions, given the long exile and historical conditions endured by the Jews. It would seem that Luther almost did not consider this a theological reading that would violate his own principles as much as an obvious and "rational" reading of history.

At the end of the day, Luther's theological consistency led him to recommendations that undermined his own faith. Beyond the charge of theological failure of nerve, we may point to two internal inconsistencies that result from his position. Kaufmann points to the following incoherencies in Luther's view:

> By ostentatiously marginalizing the Jews and making them suffer, Christians, according to the triumphalist logic of this "theology of glory," confirmed the truth of their faith and the depravity of Israel. Was Luther's faith, was his understanding of Scripture in need of these arguments? What sort of "faith" was it that was "proved" by scripture and by the course of history, by the fact of Jewish suffering? Given such strong emphasis on the demonstrable inevitability of salvation in the form of the "proof" from Scripture, where was there scope for the individual leap of faith?[22]

If faith was indeed so central to Luther, it was compromised by the intellectual and reasoned polemics that led him to refer to Jewish suffering as part of his theological scheme, leading to further enforcement of such suffering. By emphasizing the

22. Kaufmann, *Luther's Jews*, 92.

centrality of faith in this way, Kaufmann allows us to consider whether the subject of "the Jews" does not, in fact, drive a wedge between Luther's deep affirmation of faith and his hermeneutical and theological work, as it took shape around and in confrontation with "the Jews."

A second profound inconsistency emerges from the following passage, which references one of the negative recommendations of *On the Jews and Their Lies:*

> The Jews should have "all their books," "prayer books, the Talmudic texts and the whole Bible" taken from them with "not a page" left behind. For they used all their writings, even the Bible, only to blaspheme against Christ. In the case of the Jews, Luther, though a theologian of the Word, completely lost confidence in the power of God in his Word—a declaration of theological bankruptcy.[23]

It is not only that Luther fails in allowing faith to operate without needing to prove it. He also fails in letting the Bible work despite, and over and against, Jewish interpretations. Metaphysically, then, God is not powerful enough to overcome the devil; his word is not powerful enough to communicate despite conflicting interpretations. In human terms, Luther is not imbued enough with the faith and the reality of God and God's word to allow them to be and to operate, even where he himself sees no way of them achieving the desired change of heart and attitude of Jews who refuse to recognize the Christ so dear to his heart.

23. See text at chapter 5, p. 115.

6. PROTECTING CHRISTIAN IDENTITY AND AUTHENTICITY

In some ways the following point is as important, if not more important, as the hermeneutical and theological drive that impacts Luther's approach to the Jews. Affirming identity is important for any religious tradition. Identity engages the fullness of the religious personality. It thus involves fundamental drives, emotional realities, and higher theoretical considerations all brought together under the umbrella of the quest and affirmation of identity. The concerns of identity therefore draw together the psychological factors listed above with the more theoretical and theological dimensions just noted, making this a potent dimension of the religious life and of religious relations.

At the heart of the Jewish-Christian disagreement is a matter of identity. The battle over correct interpretation points to deep identity concerns. On the theoretical level: who is Israel? On the practical level: how is the continuity and identity of one community affirmed and upheld in view of the actions of another? Here is where conversion is so crucial. Conversion undermines one religious identity and suggests another. The battle over conversion is one of the most charged and painful battles between competing religious groups because it goes to the heart of personal and group identification of meaning, purpose, and identity.

The issue of conversion is central to Luther's approach to the Jews. One would think this only relates to concerns of Jewish identity. However, the concern for identity is a two-way street. It seems that a significant part of the negativity that Luther has toward Jews reverts to concerns for *Christian* identity. There are several ways in which Christian identity is potentially undermined, and Luther is sensitive to them and battles against all of them.

One way of undermining Christian identity is through conversion to Judaism. Luther had no problem thinking that Jews should convert to Christianity. But apparently the thought that Jews would engage in parallel missionary efforts geared at Christians was insupportable for him. One of the factors in Luther's increasing negativity toward Judaism seems to be knowledge of Jewish missionary efforts. Luther himself seems to have experienced these firsthand.[24] A likely reason, or a contributing factor, for Luther's changed attitudes toward Jews was his sense that his welcoming attitude had emboldened Jews and led to their own missionary activities toward Christians.[25] Luther declined Josel of Rosheim's request for support, offering the following as a reason:

> Because your people so disgracefully abuse my services to them and embark on things that we Christians cannot tolerate from them they have deprived themselves of any support that I could otherwise have given them before princes and rulers. . . . For I would be happy to do my best for you for the sake of the crucified Jew, from whom no-one shall separate me, but only if you do not use my favour to increase your stubbornness.[26]

Could this be a reference to the emboldening of Jews and their own missionary efforts?[27]

An additional dimension of affirming identity is the battle

24. See Kaufmann, *Luther's Jews*, 29–31.

25. Gritsch, *Martin Luther's Anti-Semitism*, 71; Gritsch, "Luther and the Jews," 112.

26. Kaufmann, *Luther's Jews*, 33.

27. This is how Ingemar Öberg (*Luther and World Mission*, 125) reads the story. Kaufmann (*Luther's Jews*, 31, 88–89) suggests general negative actions by Jews, such as blaspheming. The text suggests, however, an increase in stubbornness and some specific initiative that Jews have embarked upon, rather than ongoing Jewish blasphemy in the synagogue. From contemporary Jewish responses to Luther, noted above, it is clear that the Reformer raised expectations of purification of Christianity and eventual return to Judaism.

against Judaizing tendencies within the church. One of the tracts of Luther's later anti-Jewish works addresses practices of keeping the Sabbath among Christians. Luther conflates the negative attitude toward Jews with those he shows against the Sabbatarians. It is possible that the latter are a foil for a battle against the former and that Luther's anti-Jewish bias comes across in his polemic against Judaizing tendencies within the church. However, it may be that more than theological correctness is involved. The battle in both cases is to preserve Christian identity in its proper form. The entry of Jewish elements into Christian life compromises the integrity of Christian life and touches upon core concerns of identity. Luther refers to this as purity of faith.[28] Indeed, Luther saw Sabbatarians as having converted to Judaism. The battles were thus identified.[29] Luther saw Sabbatarians as Jews, regardless of their historical reality. Both Jews and Sabbatarians were thus "phantasms," expressions of Luther's theological, fearful imagination.

Concern over identity is likely one dimension of Luther's polemic against Hebraists, who engage in study with and from Jews. As Kaufmann has shown, Luther collapsed the polemics against Hebraists with his polemic against Jews.

> It was only when he had a two-pronged attack to lead—against the Jews and against Christian Hebrew scholarship that in his view did not sufficiently Christianize the Old Testament—that a dynamic was created that was capable of igniting the passion that burst forth in his writings of 1543.[30]

Here too, it seems that the argument is not simply about the correctness of interpretation. Had that been the sole concern,

28. Kaufmann, *Luther's Jews*, 89.
29. Kaufmann, *Luther's Jews*, 88–90.
30. Kaufmann, *Luther's Jews*, 124.

Luther might not have frowned upon the practices of other Reformers who enjoyed closer relations of study with Jews. The concern seems to be the preservation of Christian identity. Contact with the Jews, given the falsity of their beliefs and the stubbornness of their refusal to recognize Christ, will ultimately contaminate proper Christian understanding, thereby impacting the integrity and authenticity of Christian witness.

7. THE APOCALYPTIC DIMENSION

One additional factor is cited by scholars in understanding Luther's mentality and how it impacted his attitude toward the Jews.[31] Luther considered himself to be living at the end of time. The apocalyptic dimension heightened the tension in relation to various groups. For some, this accounts for his violent attitude to various enemies, within Christianity and beyond. This would be the framework for understanding his increasing negativity against the Jews.[32] The heightened sense of apocalypticism may also account for the change between the younger and the older Luther and for Luther renouncing his expectation of Jews converting.[33] In this view, Luther's anti-Jewish writings were "but part and parcel of an apocalyptic-polemical polemic aimed to keeping the gospel

31. I note with interest that this reasoning is absent from Kaufmann's *Luther's Jews*. Inasmuch as we seek to draw the various factors raised by scholarship into a composite picture, this picture may be augmented by the apocalyptic dimension but certainly does not require it.

32. This thesis was developed by Heiko Oberman. See Heiko A. Oberman, *Luther: Man between God and Devil* (New York: Image, 1992), 292–97; and Oberman, *Roots of Anti-Semitism*, part 3. For a discussion of this thesis, see Gritsch, *Martin Luther's Anti-Semitism*, 133–37 and the sources brought there.

33. There are different opinions as to whether Luther maintained hope and held out the possibility for conversion of Jews into his later years, or whether he renounced such a possibility. For the latter view, see Kaufmann, *Luther's Jews*, 119, 138.

afloat in the world's last ravaged hour."[34] In this view, the "period of grace has elapsed; the time of persuasion has passed; war has begun. Luther's late treatises are acts of war."[35]

The sum total of factors listed above presents us with a profile that has a certain coherence. This profile incorporates biographical, psychological, hermeneutical, theological, and identitarian dimensions into a coherent whole. Given Luther and his times, one can understand, maybe even cultivate the kind of compassion that only historical distance and perspective can offer, how Luther, despite himself and his better theological judgment, got to where he got in relation to the Jews. The ability to draw these factors into a profile, a model I call the "Luther model," allows us to consider the various factors both in the framework of reciprocal Jewish-Christian relations and more broadly as dimensions that can manifest in attitudes across religions, whichever they may be. Before engaging in these analyses, I would like to briefly note some factors that have been raised as other possibilities for Luther's changed views that, based on my reading of scholarly literature, seem to me unrelated to Luther's views of the Jews and that do not possess explanatory power in accounting for Luther's changed views.

8. DISAPPOINTMENT WITH LACK OF JEWISH CONVERSION

This "explanation" is a common trope in literature on Luther and the Jews. According to this explanation, the early Luther had hopes of converting Jews. His kind approach to them was geared at achieving this result. When his hopes were dashed,

34. Oberman, *Roots of Anti-Semitism*, 122.

35. Paul R. Hinlicky, "A Lutheran Contribution to the Theology of Judaism," *Journal of Ecumenical Studies* 31, no. 1–2 (1994): 139.

Luther turned against the Jews. The change in Luther's attitudes is thus directly related to frustrated expectations of conversion of the Jews. In this, Luther is seen like Muhammad, another religious figure who had hopes for Jewish conversion and then turned against the Jews when his hopes were dashed.[36]

It is perhaps worth following the pedigree of this theory. The earliest theorist to offer this explanation is an anonymous Jewish writer at the end of the sixteenth or beginning of the seventeenth century.[37] Jews, as we have seen, were responsive to Luther's message and historical role. As mentioned above, in various historical writings we find accounts of Luther and his views of the Jews. It is only natural that Jews would seek to account for Luther's change of heart. As the targets of Luther's conversionary hopes, it is natural for them to reconstruct changes in Luther's views in light of the degree of success or failure of his missionary attempts. This is reflected in this early historical source. It is worth noting that Jews in Luther's time, and probably for several hundred years following his time, did not actually read Luther's works. We do not possess any writing by a Jewish author that is based on a reading of the relevant sources. Rather, the story of Luther and his attitude toward Jews is known in its broad contours as part of common culture. Within this matrix, it makes sense that Jews would pride themselves on their faithfulness and see in it a reason for Luther's changed views in relation to the Jews.

In the history of scholarship, the same idea is first introduced by the Jewish historian Heinrich Graetz.[38] Graetz

36. For the comparison, see Saul S. Friedlander, "Luther and Muhammad," *Patterns of Prejudice* 5, no. 2 (1971): 6–11.

37. Debra Kaplan, "Sharing Conversations: A Jewish Polemic against Martin Luther," *Archiv fur Reformationsgeschichte* 103, no. 1 (2012): 49.

38. Heinrich Graetz, *Geschichte der Juden*, vol. 9 (Leipzig: Leiner, 1891), 303. I am unable to find reference to this crucial reasoning in the English edition, Heinrich

seems to be the first person to ever attempt to answer the question of why Luther changed his views toward the Jews. The answer he offers seems typical of Jewish mentality and its concerns. Luther failed in his hopes or efforts to convert the Jews, and this led to a change of attitude toward them.

This idea is echoed time and again.[39] Yet, there are several reasons why this theory may be questioned.[40] Had the conversion of Jews really been important for Luther, we might have expected him to engage in active missionary activity. This he did not.[41] He was content to engage in his theology and exegesis and to make these revolve around the Jews. But in the same way that real Jews were not part of his horizon, so the conversion of Jews seems to have been addressed not to the Jewish community but rather to the Christian readership.

One of the main concerns for Luther was the authenticity and sincerity of conversion.[42] Luther took exception to superficial policies that sought to appease political (Roman) powers and to change the status of Jews in society. He desired a genuine conversion. He did not seek broad converts to the religion, but deep and sincere ones. This too would suggest

Graetz, *History of the Jews* (Philadelphia: Jewish Society of America, 1956), 550ff. Graetz's position is referenced by Christian Wiese ("'Let His Memory Be Holy to Us': Jewish Interpretations of Martin Luther from the Enlightenment to the Holocaust," *Leo Baeck Institute Yearbook* 54 [2009]: 121), where it is contrasted with Jost's history of 1828, which refers only to the earlier Luther and ignores the later.

39. Typical is Gritsch, "Luther and the Jews," 113; Gritsch, *Martin Luther's Anti-Semitism*, 139. See also Jaroslav Pelikan, "Luther Comes to the New World," in *Luther and the Dawn of the Modern Era*, ed. Heiko A. Oberman (Leiden: Brill, 1974), 9.

40. The absence of this theory from Kaufmann's *Luther's Jews* is significant. Kaufmann titles chapter 4 "Hopes Disappointed," referring to the disappointment that Jews did not convert. However, other than a passing reference to "disappointment" on p. 83, itself placed within quotation marks, this does not seem to figure in his telling of Luther's story. By contrast, his description provides several good reasons for why such disappointment should not be considered a part of the story. See also Kaufmann, "Luther and the Jews," 87.

41. Kaufmann, "Luther and the Jews," 97.

42. Kaufmann, "Luther and the Jews," 97.

that broad conversion of Jews was not a priority or a program.

The later Luther did not consider conversion as a key solution to the Jewish problem. Had conversion been uppermost on his mind and the source of his disappointment with the Jews, we would have expected some residue and continuing hope for their conversion, perhaps even forced conversion. At the very least, conversion should have been an option that was made available for those Jews who were open to it.[43] This suggests that while the Jews were central to his theological thinking, their actual conversion was not an immediate goal. Accordingly, it should not be seen as the reason for changes in his attitude.

9. FAILING HEALTH

Some have suggested that Luther's failing health in his old age accounts for his changed attitude toward the Jews.[44] Surely, if there was a personal and psychological component that impacted his overall theological orientation, one cannot totally exclude the workings of the body and his ill health on his psychological attitude.[45] Nevertheless, the composite picture above has a coherence that cannot be reduced to a medical explanation, a coherence that allows us to recount the different stages of his attitude to the Jews as an unfolding con-

43. Oberman (*Roots of Anti-Semitism*, 113, 123), who is the proponent of the apocalyptic Luther, does consider conversion as an option up to the end of Luther's career, even if only for the few. However, conversion plays a very minor role in the teachings and recommendations of the later Luther and may even have been considered by him as an option that was no longer viable. Cf. Kaufmann, *Luther's Jews*, 119.

44. See Lindberg, "Tainted Greatness," 18–19.

45. In this spirit, one can recognize the "understanding" offered by Kaufmann (*Luther's Jews*, 96) as a contributing factor within a broader matrix, but not as a standalone explanation for Luther's views.

tinuum, not a consequence of external forces that disrupted its coherent unfolding. The medical explanation might provide the physical framework within which the processes described above took place and were intensified.

10. ACCEPTANCE OF PREVAILING OPINIONS

The possibility that the change in Luther's views can be ascribed to existing conventions or views of the Jews lacks explanatory power. If the early Luther did not share prevailing opinions, why would the later Luther have done so. Even if the meaning of the change of his view amounts to buying into typical medieval prejudice against the Jews, there must be some reason why ideas that he rejected in his youth would be adopted in his old age. As there was nothing inherently rational or convincing in the ideas he rejected in 1523, we must seek the answer elsewhere.

11. JEWS AS STAND-IN FOR PAPISTS

George Lindbeck, in an article that seeks to sidestep the problem of "Luther and the Jews" by recasting the essential Luther into certain catechetical works that are devoid of anti-Judaic elements, makes an additional apologetic move. Lindbeck argues that when Luther speaks against the Jews, it is not the Jews he has in mind. The Jews in Luther's writings are a stand-in for papists.[46] The later vitriol was a by-product of anti-papal venom. While it is true that Luther found significant overlap between these two enemies and could even speak of one in light of the other, it is hard

46. George Lindbeck, "Martin Luther and the Rabbinic Mind," in *Understanding the Rabbinic Mind: Essays on the Hermeneutic of Max Kadushin*, ed. Peter Ochs (Atlanta: Scholars, 1990), 162.

to reduce the centrality of Jews in Luther's works to mascots for Catholics. The negative presence of Jews is too germane to his theological work, and its reality too strong, to be considered as merely a stand-in for papists.

5.

Recognizing the Reciprocal Challenge

Discussions of "Luther and the Jews" have focused in the main on Luther, not on the Jews. The focus has been on the novelty of the Reformer's approach to Jews and then on his change of heart, leading to some of the most virulent anti-Semitic expressions in the history of Christian literature. As a result, the study of Luther has been undertaken in the framework of historical study and curiosity—or, more often, in the context or within the horizons of contemporary Jewish-Christian relations. Luther on Judaism has become a problem for contemporary Lutherans, and the study of Luther in some way grapples with this problem. No contemporary author can refer to the problem without in some way taking a stand—be it a critical stand or an attempt to better understand Luther in context—on the problems generated, both historically and in terms of intergroup relations, by Luther's positions on Jews, as well as on other religious groups.

As stated above, Jews on the whole have avoided engaging Luther as a significant dialogue partner or as a resource for contemporary Jewish-Christian relations. Luther is a problem, not a resource or a lesson.

In what follows I offer a complementary approach. I do not seek in any way to minimize Luther's negativity; nor do I suggest any reciprocity that would somehow justify or detract from the severity of his positions. What I do seek to do is to consider how the witness of Luther the anti-Semite can address contemporary Jewish-Christian relations—and, more broadly, relations between different faith communities—in ways that bear lessons that are relevant for all. Typically, Luther is treated either in isolation, as a person with particular circumstances, or as part of a larger history of negative Christian attitudes toward Judaism. The question is never asked in what way Luther represents problems, spiritual illnesses that have the potential to affect believers of all faiths and potentially in all times. Luther cannot be divorced from the history of Christian anti-Judaism, and his role in mixing anti-Semitism and religion with the eventual harmful consequences to the Jewish community is singular. However, if we look at the deeper roots of "what went wrong" with Luther, from our ideal and peace-seeking perspective, the answers are not unique. Rather, they point to dynamics that can exist at any time and that can manifest in any religion. In the same way that "religious genius" can speak across traditions, so the faults that attach to a great personality can also teach lessons that transcend the particular of the person and his circumstances.

Luther on Judaism can teach us fundamental lessons of what to avoid in relations between faith communities and traditions. Those lessons are of broader universal significance and as such also apply to Jews. In other words, there are circumstances under which Jews could commit the same errors that Luther committed. Theoretically, they could take stands in relation to Christians or members of other faiths similar to those taken by Luther. There is always the potential that actions follow theoretical views and that actions of a similar kind, recommended by Luther with regards to Jews, might be enacted by Jews toward Christians or others. In one way, it makes all the difference that wide-scale atrocities were committed by those who listened to Luther with regard to Jews, in ways that cannot invite comparison or reciprocity. In another way, it may matter less than we think if we realize that there is reciprocity of attitudes, and that in some small measure, no matter how small, actions have been carried out that suggest some kind of reciprocity. The reason why essentially quantitative comparisons should not matter is twofold. First, translating negative religious attitudes toward another group into policy and action is a matter of the conjunction of religion, or ideology, and power. Such conjunctions change as political circumstances change. What was unthinkable yesterday could become reality tomorrow. Which leads to the second and related point. Religions are not measured only in light of negativity and hostility as these are expressed in practice. Religions matter for the personalities they form, the ideas they instill, and the training of heart and mind they achieve. Even if negativity is curbed by political and social forces, negativity of the mind may be as detrimental to the well-being of society and the proper functioning of religion as when religion becomes violent and aggressive to the other. Consequently, when talking of Luther and "what went wrong," we must focus on the internal, subjective, ideological, and theological dimensions, rather than only on the outward, political, social, and practical expressions of the negativity of the mind. From this perspective, and possibly only from this perspective, Luther has important lessons to teach members of other faiths.

The present reflection is being carried out from a particular point in time and place and with full awareness of how present circumstances reflect back on the core dynamics operative in Luther and his view of Jews. The problem of "Luther and the Jews" came to full light following the Holocaust, when one could no longer avoid the negative and harmful legacy of Luther and simply prefer the "good," younger Luther. Adolf von Harnack posed the question, "Who is truly bold enough to reanimate 'the complete Luther?'"—in other words, to give equal weight to all parts of his writings.[1] The need to confront the full Luther has led to soul-searching and revisiting the legacy of the Reformer and its personal and theological roots. The historical context has been conditioned primarily by the Holocaust and secondarily by the new reality of Jewish return to Israel's homeland.[2] Within this context, the focus has been on the responsibility and self-correction of the Christian side. This has yielded revisiting Luther as well as multiple public apologies of Lutheran Churches. Jews have been recipients of the process, at best engaging in the quest for redeeming relations with Lutherans and Christians. The discussion has not demanded they take stock of anything that requires addressing within Jewish attitudes to Christianity. The following discussion does just that.

1. Thomas Kaufmann, *Luther's Jews: A Journey into Anti-Semitism* (Oxford: Oxford University Press, 2017), 157.

2. See Darrell Jodock, ed., *Covenantal Conversations: Christians in Dialogue with Jews and Judaism* (Minneapolis: Fortress Press, 2008), 2–3. The book has a distinctly Lutheran orientation, though it does not address the specific legacy of Martin Luther.

The circumstances that justify making Luther, in his shortcomings and moral failures, speak to a Jewish audience in a movement of self-examination are particular to the State of Israel at seventy and to some of the manifestations of Judaism that it allows. To be clear, the actions that call for such self-examination are undertaken by a minority that is so small it has no representative standing. Yet, this unrepresentative minority does share much broader commonalities of mind, attitude, thought, and theological positioning within Jewish circles. If the root of problems between groups are in the mind, heart, and teaching cultivated by a tradition, then the lessons of what goes wrong in one tradition when bad thinking translates into action are relevant for another.

The particular context that has led me to this line of thinking has to do with the rise of anti-Christian sentiments in present-day Israel. One extreme expression of this is the arson carried out in the Church of Loaves and Fishes at Tabgha.[3] Two youths set fire to church buildings, inscribing on the complex's walls a quote from the Jewish prayer book. The message was that Christianity was idolatrous and that it should be eradicated. The graffiti also assumed that the youths were empowered to act on this understanding. The theological position translated to immediate action toward Christians. The situation was nonrepresentative and was widely condemned. Condemnation focused on group relations and on the fact that these youths were in no way empowered to carry out their activities, nor is there any instruction to take action in uprooting or harming Christians and their institutions. However, the core of the battle relates to the very notion of one religion viewing the other as idolatry. The

3. "Arson Attack," in "Church of the Multiplication," Wikipedia, http://tinyurl.com/yc4jw3re.

deeper attitudes may or may not beget harmful actions. But they poison attitudes toward other faiths and impede genuine spiritual sharing between faiths.

The paradox is that Jews in Luther's native Germany held on to a view for centuries that considered Christian worship legitimate for Christians.[4] Much of this consensus has eroded in present-day Israel, with the view of Christianity as idolatry gaining the upper hand and becoming near-consensus. Along with such delegitimation of Christianity comes a host of minor expressions of contempt and petty violence. Once again, even if these are carried out by minority and fringe groups, disaffected youth and the like, these draw on broader theoretical and emotional attitudes that are found among faithful Jews. All this leads me to consider that, in fact, the similarity and reciprocity between the problems we encounter in the study of Luther's views of Judaism and some present-day Jewish views of Christianity are significant enough to apply lessons from Luther to other contexts and to make them speak to the contemporary Jewish-Christian reality.

It may be that I am particularly sensitive to the issue and may even be placing a magnifying glass on it where many of my coreligionists would prefer to simply ignore and dismiss such incidents and attitudes. My own engagement with and response to the arson at Tabgha is relevant. This incident led to my extensive engagement in reparation work, both physical and educational. Recognizing the roots of the problem as theological in view of the graffiti featuring verses from the Jewish prayer book, I gathered a group of rabbis to support a crowdfunding campaign, aimed primarily at Jews, to support

4. See Eugene Korn, "Rethinking Christianity: Rabbinic Positions and Possibilities," in *Jewish Theology and World Religions*, ed. Alon Goshen-Gottstein and Eugene Korn (Oxford: Littman Library of Jewish Civilization, 2012), 197–202.

the rebuilding of the church. The point was more than gaining public support for the monks and condemnation for the arsonists. Recognizing the theological roots of the problem, the campaign sought to bring to light Jewish voices from the halakic (legal) tradition that affirmed Christianity's nonidolatrous status. It was thus intended as an educational effort, by means of a public-relations and crowdfunding campaign. For me, the most important achievement of the campaign was that in many online forums, lively discussions occurred where participants were exposed for the first time to classical and contemporary rabbinic voices that legitimate Christianity.

Let me relate another anecdote that will explain why I consider there to be similarities in circumstances between present-day Israel and Luther's Middle Age context. There is an organization in Israel called Lehava, which seeks to minimize intermarriage between Jews and non-Jews. Its founder, a gentleman by the name of Benzion Gupstein, has spoken in favor of setting fire to churches and against the right of Christians to be in Israel, at the very least in theoretical terms.[5] I recall a meeting with Bishop Boulos Marcuzzo, a Catholic bishop in Galilee, where the bishop expressed his concern and horror with the possibility that Gupstein's views might infect others and translate into action. To argue that this Gupstein is a fringe phenomenon, condemned by most Israelis, religious as well as secular, would be beside the point. After all, history has taught us that today's minority can become tomorrow's majority. I believe the bishop's fears are well-founded, though not specifically because tomorrow Christians will be expelled and their houses of worship razed to the ground. They are well-founded because someone like himself, who

5. Chaim Levinson, "Israeli Extremist Group Leader Calls for Torching of Churches," *Haaretz*, August 6, 2015, http://tinyurl.com/y827k3zl.

has fully integrated the processes of *Nostra Aetate* and who has repositioned himself in relation to Judaism, is able to recognize unreformed religion and how the propagation of hateful and exclusionary attitudes not only undermines positive and constructive relations but can also become a danger for everyone's well-being. The danger is real. Accordingly, when Luther's horrible recommendations in *On the Jews and Their Lies* are read in present-day Israel, they cannot be read only from a hermeneutic of accusation, where Jewish victims accuse Christian perpetrators for centuries of Jewish suffering. They also have to be read from a hermeneutic of introspection and self-examination, seeking to recognize that "what went wrong" in one religious tradition may also go wrong in another; in fact, the seeds of what can go wrong are already there today. Some of them have sprouted.

In important ways, the challenge that Jews, as well as others, are faced with is the same in qualitative terms (even if not in quantitative terms) as that faced by Christians in general and, in our case, by Lutherans. The response to Harnack's challenge of reanimating the full Luther involves a critical reading of tradition, historical contextualization, and an attempt to purify tradition in view of the harmful consequences of certain attitudes and theological positions. A similar challenge faces Judaism, and it therefore has what to learn from looking at Luther.

We have already seen that the view of another tradition is often a view projected from within. We have recognized that Luther's Judaism was a projection of his internal realities, concerns, and ambiguities. Jews were mirrors for Luther, not real relationships or personalities. It may be suggested that Luther—that is, the anti-Judaic and anti-Semitic persona—can play a similar role for Jewish reflection. Albert

Friedlander points us in this direction when he says that in the same way that the Jew served for Luther as an image of himself, in dealing with Luther and working our way through the chaos, we are also working through something in ourselves.[6]

6. Albert Friedlander, "Martin Luther und wir Juden," in *Die Juden und Martin Luther—Martin Luther und die Juden*, ed. H. Kremers (Neukirchen: Neukirchener, 1985), 290.

6.

Applying the "Luther Model" Within

Let us now work through each of the components of the "Luther model" and consider how it does, or how it might, find expression in some contemporary Jewish attitudes toward Christianity.

1. LACK OF CONTACT AND NO MEANINGFUL FIRSTHAND KNOWLEDGE

This may be considered the foundation of inadequate and negative relations with the religious other. No knowledge means no friendship, no commitment to another person.[1] The consequences of lack of personal acquaintance are more far-reaching than limited knowledge of real people and their real lived religion. Ultimately, it impacts the possibility of love as a foundation of the spiritual life and, in the case of the Christianity, as the greatest command. To love, one must have a real relationship. One cannot love some abstraction.

1. On the theoretical possibility and significance of interreligious friendship, see Alon Goshen-Gottstein, ed., *Friendship across Religions: Theological Perspectives on Interreligious Friendship* (Lanham, MD: Lexington, 2015).

How can Jews be loved if they are not part of society and if one does not have real Jewish friends? The big change that has occurred ever since emancipation of the Jews, particularly since World War II, is that Jews and Christians in most of the Western world have become friends. Friendship and coexistence provide the foundation for revisiting Jewish-Lutheran relations.[2] Such friendship was unimaginable in Luther's days.

Sadly, there are parts of the Jewish world, especially the Orthodox and especially in Israel, that share the fundamental "friendless" reality in relation to members of other faiths. Again, sadly, when it comes to Christianity, this reality of "friendlessness" is further compounded by other aspects of the model that we see operating in the case of Luther's attitude to the Jews. One of the negative side effects of creating a Jewish, or Jewish-majority, society is that all too often there is no opportunity or motivation to encounter members of other religions. This allows ideas of yesteryear to continue informing the image of the religious other. The most extreme consequences of such a social reality result in acts of hostility and enmity, small (spitting) or significant (such as the arson described above, even if it is an exceptional expression of the same tendency).

To recognize that we as Jews can harbor similar attitudes born of similar social conditions as those that characterize Luther's view of the Jews is sobering. Surely, there are significant differences. Jews in the Middle Ages lived on the fringes of society. Their reality, in many ways, was a shadow reality, analogous to today's Roma people. But social estrangement does not require social marginalization. It only requires an ordering of society around centers of common interest,

2. Darrell Jodock, ed., *Covenantal Conversations: Christians in Dialogue with Jews and Judaism* (Minneapolis: Fortress Press, 2008), 3.

which creates de facto homogenic communities, self-imposed and ideologically organized "ghettos" of common concern and shared identity.

The problem is significantly complicated when otherness is both social and theological. When there is theological otherness due to differing faiths, social communion helps offset negativity that could be introduced from the theological realm. However, in the absence of real relationships and friendships on the ground, the image of the other is exclusively theological and conditioned by theological perspectives and categories. The more this is so, the more the other loses his reality as a person and becomes simply a manifestation of the principles projected upon him, representing theological difference. Common humanity gives way to the projections of theological alterity.

In the absence of real relationship, imagination and fear set in. One expression of this is the certainty that the other wishes you ill. We have noted Luther's fear of Jews, a direct consequence of lack of real relationships. More broadly, Luther was certain that Jews wish Christians ill.

> They wish us every kind of harm with curses, slanders and spitting beyond imagining. They wish that violence and wars, terror and every type of misery should overtake us accursed Goyim. They do this cursing every Saturday openly in their synagogues and daily in their own homes. They teach, encourage and accustom their children to do these things from their childhood onwards so that they will remain bitter, virulent and vicious enemies of Christians.[3]

Naturally, "As in water the face is to face, So the heart of man to man."[4] One's attitude to the other becomes the basis

3. Thomas Kaufmann, *Luther's Jews: A Journey into Anti-Semitism* (Oxford: Oxford University Press, 2017), 112.

4. Prov 27:19.

of the other's response. Hate breeds hates and fear breeds fear. It is not the case that Jews loved Christians, who in turn hated them. Negativity may well have been reciprocal, even if uneven in its social expressions.[5] Jewish negativity would have been further fueled by earlier manifestations of the same dynamic in relation to the other as it found expression in negative portrayals of non-Jews in the Talmud.[6] Yet, such mutual vilification and the reciprocity of suspicion and hate are all the consequence of lack of relationship, the absence of friendship.

Perhaps the most extreme form of othering is Luther's demonization of Jews and his claim that they are affiliated with the devil.[7] While we may well point out the harmful historical consequences of dehumanization and demonization of the other, we must also be prepared to revisit our foundational literature in search of similar attitudes. A disempowered and persecuted minority may well find consolation—moreover, may well be considered justified—in portraying its enemies and all those who are other to it as cosmically and metaphysically associated with other sources of life and spiritual vitality. To claim that non-Jews draw their vitality from "the other side," as some kabbalists would have it, is to project otherness onto the metaphysical realm.[8] It is also a way of answering how Jews could suffer in the hands of others. Those others draw their force and power from forces of darkness, not from the Divine. Such a metaphysical claim is a way of affirming identity and separateness, thereby both justify-

5. In Luther's work on Shem Hamephorash, he quotes the Jewish counter-gospel *Toledot Yeshu*. Literary and "historical" sources reinforce a negativity founded upon distance, suspicion, and hate.

6. Sacha Stern, *Jewish Identity in Early Rabbinic Writings* (Leiden: Brill, 1994), especially chapter 1.

7. Kaufmann, *Luther's Jews*, 88, 118.

8. To claim that non Jews draw their vitality form the other side, see Elliot R. Wolfson, *Venturing Beyond: Law and Morality in Kabbalistic Mysticism* (Oxford: Oxford University Press, 2006), 73–80, 90–107, 135–54.

ing and possibly perpetuating a history of separateness that includes suffering and persecution as constituent elements. In the same way that we can understand how Luther got where he got to, we can understand how certain metaphysical associations accompany Jewish views of non-Jews or of other religions. But when we view the harmful consequences of dehumanization and demonization of another, whatever the reason or theoretical foundations for it may be, must we not also recognize some aspect of ourselves in such activities and projections? Luther allows us to view such negativity with a distance afforded by looking at an "enemy" of some historical distance and through the ability to recognize the multiplicity of forces that converge to create the entire relational model, which is fed by lack of real contact[9] and culminates in demonization of the other.[10] Once we recognize the model in its entirety, we are not free to ignore the possibility that it is also present within us.

If Jews served for Luther as internal mirrors, and if, as Friedlander invites us, Luther should serve a similar role for Jews, we are led to the next level of considering how otherness operates within our religious psyche and imagination, a possibility that is much enhanced by the other lacking concrete reality and the commanding presence of real relationships and friendships.

Because for Luther, the Jew was not a personal reality but a construct, a projection, a phantasm, the Jew could operate not only externally but also internally. Accordingly, the Jew

9. To be sure, persecution and the various forms in which many Jews experienced Christian society are very real, even if they point to another aspect of reality. We can readily recognize how these could have contributed to a dualistic view of the other and his demonization.

10. This relates to a more fundamental issue, that of dualistic thinking. We shall touch upon it below. Significantly, it is an important dimension of spiritual literature and the battle for purity and spiritual evolution that it features.

becomes an aspect, a theoretical possibility of a way of being. If so, every person has a Jew within, and the Jew within must be confronted in the process of spiritual growth. The progression from Old to New Testament may further enhance the process of internal conversion and the quest for dealing with the Jew within.[11] At its most extreme, this interiorization of the "Jew" actually has spiritual potential. Distance from the real person and sublimation of the negativity associated with the Jew to a spiritual aspect that everyone has within themselves could be a strategy for containing and limiting harmful attitudes. These are symbolized, internalized, and made part of oneself. Yet, this very move is not only conditioned on lack of relationship with the objective "Jew," it also has the potential of returning to concrete reality and translating into social negativity.

Let us consider the mirror situation. The suggestion that there is a "non-Jew" within is not a far one in certain kinds of mystical literature. R. Abraham Joshua Heschel was a great Hasidic luminary of the eighteenth and early nineteenth century.[12] In his Torah commentary *Ohev Yisrael*, he discusses the biblical passages of Deuteronomy 25, where we are commanded to remember Israel's historical and metaphysical archenemy, Amalek.[13] He writes:

> It is still incumbent upon us to break the force and power of the wicked Haman, who is of the seed of Amalek that is hidden within the heart of each and every person of Israel, individually

11. For expressions and consequences of this attitude, see Heiko A. Oberman, *The Roots of Anti-Semitism in the Age of Renaissance and Reformation* (Philadelphia: Fortress Press, 1984), 106–7, 110ff.

12. The famous twentieth-century Jewish theologian who carries the same name is a grandson.

13. On Amalek, see Alon Goshen-Gottstein, "Judaism: The Battle for Survival, the Struggle for Compassion," in *The Religious Other: Hostility, Hospitality and the Hope of Human Flourishing*, ed. Alon Goshen-Gottstein (Lanham, MD: Lexington, 2015), 31–32.

> as well as collectively. That is, that each one of us, the people of God, should annihilate and uproot the evil that is concealed within him.[14]

Finding the "other" and the enemy within may be "cleaner" in terms of containing it within a spiritual context and limiting its impact to the world within. Yet, the containment of "the non-Jew within the Jew" cannot be considered foolproof. There is nothing inherent in the concept or somehow representative of Judaism as a religion that has inherent self-restraint in relation to the other. Rather, such restraint and the fact that negativity does not spill out to the real world are functions of power relations and concrete opportunities. These could always change. What we face today, as Jews, is the possibility that given shifts in power relations, some of the negative attitudes that have found expression in relation to us could be expressed by us toward others.

Despite some appeal of interiorizing otherness, the possibility of sublimating otherness as part of a spiritual worldview and praxis is contingent on lack of concrete and meaningful relationships. It is not possible for me to imagine myself transcending a part of myself, identified as negative, when that part is identified with someone to whom I feel close, whom I respect, and who represents positive spiritual values. At the end of the day, the only way forward in Jewish-Christian relations, and in the globalized world of encounters between faiths and communities, is to transform othering through real encounters with the other. This, and this alone, will undermine the foundations of hatred and negativity that affect in some way and at some point in time the relations between members of all faith communities.

There are two concluding thoughts I would like to offer

14. R. Abraham Joshua Heschel, "Zachor and Purim," in *Ohev Yisrael*, 110.

on this component of the model. The problem of othering, based on lack of relationship, is nowadays a central component of intergroup relations. More than Jews and Christians, it concerns the image of the Muslim in today's world. It matters little that there are negative expressions of Islam that feed this image. The fact is that this image flourishes on lack of contact, as well as upon partial and wrong information. The situation that applied to Luther's relations to the Jews is actually an expression of a broader contemporary syndrome in global relations between faith communities. Recognizing the dynamic through the opportunities provided by the study of a great figure at significant historical distance, allows us to question our own contemporary attitudes.

A second expression of the same problem is more nuanced and less obvious, but I believe very prevalent. The present discussion recognizes how the State of Israel positions us in a new historical context from which to engage in an evaluation of Jewish-Christian relations in relation to the "Luther model." This new historical situation also provides new opportunities for projection, for ignorance, and even for extending old anti-Jewish and anti-Semitic attitudes. Some of Luther's heirs are affiliated with a vision of an ideal world, social justice, and overcoming oppression. This vision is related to political realities in Israel-Palestine and increasingly feeds into a negative view of Israelis, and even Jews. The politicization of Jewish tradition through the Jewish state ends up providing new channels for projection. In the absence of real relationships, and very often in the absence of knowledge of complexities on the ground, facile projections of a political nature, even if grounded in goodwill and possibly well-intentioned, fall into the same trap that Luther's projections on Jews did. The conflict over interpretation of divine word is replaced by a conflict over land and inheritance. Images of occupation fulfill the function of othering, and old attitudes find new expressions. I imagine the projection of deep-seated anti-Semitic attitudes on to contemporary political realities and the continuing view of the Jew as a mirror for other concerns, now seen through a political lens,[15] are at least as widespread as the harmful dynamics considered above in relation to some contemporary Jewish attitudes toward Christians. Wherever such negativity is encountered, we must return to the foundations of the model of estrangement represented by Luther. Even if ideology and the good cause of others' rights have replaced the weighty mandates of theology, and even if the image of occupation has replaced the wrong reading of the biblical text, the same dynamics of othering and projection still occur. There is only one way of moving forward. Only by making relationships real, understanding individuals in their settings and realities, and advancing an agenda of friendship across difference can the various harmful consequences of isolation, projection, and othering be overcome.

2. KNOWLEDGE OF THE OTHER

The dynamics of Jewish-Christian relations and Christianity's growth from Judaism, the sharing of a common canon, and the hermeneutics of Old Testament interpretation were decisive for Luther's views of Judaism. Luther had no room for a Judaism that stands on its own, independent of Christian absorption and incorporation of Old Testament legacy. Religious pluralism was not a value that was known to Luther,

15. See Betsy Halpern Amaru, "Martin Luther and Jewish Mirrors," *Jewish Social Studies* 46, no. 2 (1984): 101.

and the only way that Jews could be seen was through his interpretive lens, which read the New Testament into the Old Testament, the proper Jewish scripture. All later religious works of the rabbinic and later periods that actually define Judaism over and against Christianity had no legitimacy in Luther's eyes.

The profound issue that continues to challenge Jewish-Christian relations is the issue of mutual legitimacy and validation. It was only after the Holocaust that Christians were able to make the decisive break with the tradition that Luther belonged to and that did not allow for the continuing validity of Judaism. The Catholic Church in its landmark *Nostra Aetate* was followed by other churches in affirming the enduring validity of Judaism, independent of the Christian message.

This has led to an important challenge, one that has not been fully met to date: understanding Judaism and studying it on its terms, rather than on Christian terms. All too often, Christians continue to view Judaism as Old Testament Judaism. This has implications for curricula, for training of priests, and for religious and interreligious education. Even if the hostility of Luther is a thing of the past, the positioning of Christianity in relation to Judaism and the consequent recognition of Judaism in the fullness of its practices and scriptures remain a desideratum of the future. Judaism is often known in its distinctiveness, independent of Christian eyes and witness, only by specialists and those leaders and practitioners who have enjoyed real relationships with Jewish individuals and communities. The challenge of getting to know Judaism on its own terms remains an educational and pastoral challenge on the Christian side. The reality that Luther represents cannot be said to be a thing of the past.

The same is probably even truer for Judaism in its view of Christianity. Aside from specialists or those who share common living circumstances and friendship with Christians, such as in the Jewish diaspora, Jews exhibit an alarmingly high rate of ignorance with reference to Christianity. Some of this is due to general religious illiteracy. I am thinking here of the Jewish religious community, especially Orthodoxy, both in Israel and abroad. Learning another religion is on the whole discouraged, whether as an unnecessary distraction from what matters most—Jewish religious studies—or worse as something forbidden, where Christianity is seen as idolatry. If Christians read the Old Testament as part of their Scripture, many Jews will avoid reading the New Testament on principled ground. The same holds true for later Christian writings, liturgy, theology, and so forth. Christianity is known only in its broadest contours, typically through secondhand literature and literature that recycles old polemical arguments that keep the two religions distinct, with the obvious superiority of Judaism. In an atmosphere of polite neighborly relations and substantive disengagement, as one might characterize the diaspora Orthodox experience, the damage is less great. Lack of knowledge serves an ideology of withdrawal within the community and avoidance of exposure to the outside. Cordial relations of day-to-day life somehow provide a counterpoint.

Ignorance and illiteracy in the Israeli context could have a far more pernicious effect. If Christianity is only known through secondhand polemical sources, to some extent the equivalent of Anton Margaritha's presentation of Judaism, wrong information and an unsympathetic and nonunderstanding view of the other can lead to harmful consequences.[16] Seen in isolation, lack of direct knowledge of Christian life and Christian sources may not be the most harmful dimension of a contemporary Jewish attitude to Christianity. When taken in combination with other dimensions of the "Luther model," lack of direct knowledge of Christianity and its sources can play a very destructive role in relations and in society.[17]

There is a further dimension to lack of knowledge of the other when it comes to Jewish knowledge of Christianity. The second half of the twentieth century ushered in a new era in Jewish-Christian relations. Beginning with the Catholic Church and extending to other churches, including the Lutheran Church, the attitude to Judaism has been thoroughly revised. At core, Judaism is viewed as a valid religion, no longer a zero-sum game between two competing versions of the one story. Numerous documents have been issued by

16. A recent incident is telling. An Israeli youth who had just found his way back to Jewish observance visited the town of Uman, where the great Hasidic master R. Nachman of Breslav is buried. Locals, in what is likely an intended offense to Hasidim, had put up a huge cross at a point that is frequented during an annual pilgrimage. The Hasidim had the wisdom to absorb the intended insult and not respond. This youth, however, decided to tear it down, expressing thereby whatever he had been taught about Christianity. Shortly thereafter the municipality of Uman tore down various buildings and structures that did not have building licenses and that were of interest to the Hasidim. They had been willing to turn a blind eye previously, but facing religious abuse, retaliated by enforcing law. This is a small example of a widespread mentality and how it can ultimately backfire in terms of the interests of the Jewish community. On this incident, see "Israeli Man Arrested in Ukraine for Desecrating Cross," *Jewish Telegraphic Agency*, January 4, 2017, http://tinyurl.com/ydg3tkvv; "Uproar in Uman: 'Kohanim Bridge' Removed from Tzion of Rav Nachman or Breslov," Jewish Tidbits, January 26, 2017, http://tinyurl.com/ycm2otyl. The connection between the two events was made in Israeli ultraorthodox media.

17. I recognize this discussion makes the assumption that a reading of another culture and close knowledge will of necessity be positive and serve relationships. This is of course not guaranteed. A sympathetic appreciation of another religion requires more than firsthand exposure. For someone who is convinced of the lack of value of Christianity, simply studying it will not provide an antidote to a negative view of the tradition. However, a considered approach to Christianity could profile dimensions of the tradition that provide inspiration and enhancement to shared values and a common spiritual quest. At the very least, knowledge of changes in church teachings would surely have a beneficial effect for relations between the religions.

all churches. Heavy media coverage of three papal visits to the Holy Land provided important opportunities for these changes to become widely acknowledged. Yet, significant sectors of Orthodoxy refuse to acknowledge or take note of these advances in relations. The responses range from ignoring them to highlighting specific objections to reciprocal recognition. The two most common objections are faithfulness to the memory of suffering and persecution endured by Jews at the hands of Christians, and the legal status of Christianity as idolatry, hence an illegitimate religion. Both will be dealt with below. Consequently, the attitude of continued suspicion endures, fed by ongoing concern due to Christian missionary work, also to be discussed below. One of the ways in which the "Luther model"—which presents the coming together of the various factors that lead to estrangement, distance, and othering—is useful is to recognize the distinct elements and how they operate individually and in concert. Lack of knowledge of developments on the Christian side is intimately linked with other concerns that provide the cause for what is ultimately a willful ignoring of theological changes in the attitude of Christian churches toward Judaism. As suggested, such ignoring is closely related to the attachment to, or respect for, the pain and persecution suffered by Jews in Christian hands.

3 AND 4. PERSONAL HURT AND OFFENSE, AS CONSEQUENCE OF DEEP RELIGIOUS ENGAGEMENT, AND PERSONAL TRAUMA AND PERSONAL FEARS

Relations between groups and across religions are not only about ideas. Because religion touches the deepest places in a person, religious divides touch the deepest depths and generate the greatest pain. Pain is a significant and unavoidable dimension of religious relations. It conditions theological attitudes and is fed by them. We have noted how Luther's personal hurt and pain fed his view of Jews. These views ended up generating further pain and anguish, as they produced in him a state of fear and anxiety in relation to Jews. Ideas, beliefs, and emotions intersect. Memory carries them forward. One formative experience, the report of Jesus being called "the hung one," comes up time and again in Luther's discourse, suggesting how pain and memory interact. Painful memory appears repeatedly, as trauma, if you will, and further conditions attitudes that in turn reinforce this sense of pain, along with the indignity, insult, and other emotional dimensions that attach to it.

Considering pain and hurt as dimensions that condition Jewish attitudes to Christianity, one realizes how extensive such pain is. Luther is part of that pain. So are generations of persecutions and a history of painful memory. This memory generates distrust, which remains an important component that leads to avoidance of friendship and contact and to the inability in certain sectors to recognize changes in Christian teaching. Pain cannot be handled theologically. It requires its own processes of containment and healing. Progress in making the other real can aid in coping with pain and memory; so can recognition of change. But pain and memory require their own processes of what Saint John Paul II called "purification of memory." This is a broader challenge facing all relations that carry the pain of yesteryear.[18]

In objective terms, Jews have likely suffered more in the

18. The subject was examined from the perspective of different religions in Alon Goshen-Gottstein, ed., *Memory and Hope: Forgiveness, Healing and Interfaith Relations* (Lanham, MD: Lexington, 2015).

hands of Christians than the hurt they themselves caused. Yet, as the story of Luther teaches us, it is ultimately irrelevant to compare pain. One man's pain, even based on an incident or encounter that is not of great enormity in the grand scheme of things, can have lasting effects and consequences. It is a mind-boggling thought to consider what long-term effects on Jewish lives and Jewish-Christian relations several small incidents have had. Consider as a thought exercise how Luther might have related to Jews and what the effect on Jewish well-being might have been had a different kind of discourse characterized the Jewish approach to Christian faith. To be clear, I am not suggesting that Jews are to blame or have brought upon themselves something they deserved through the instrument of Martin Luther. I only wish to point out that we cannot underestimate either the place of pain, hurt, and insult in shaping attitudes or the need for addressing the emotional component of relationships as part of advancing relations between faith communities that carry the memory of past hurt. Unless pain is dealt with and trust built, one will lack the will to consider lessons in the theological dimension that shapes relations and gives them the objective contours that justify and perpetuate religious difference, competition, and conflict.

5. THEOLOGICAL AND SCRIPTURAL DIFFERENCE

The greater part of Luther's attacks on Judaism was undertaken through the medium of scriptural interpretation and in the framework of theological argumentation. The Jewish-Christian conflict was thus objectified, lending it an air of truth and objectivity, and placing it, to a large extent, beyond the realm of reasoned discourse and the possibility of healing and repair. Once we move to the domain of theology, and polemical interreligious dispute, reciprocity, misunderstanding, and misrepresentation increase. Both sides engage in the process more or less to the same degree, whether in the framework of an explicit polemic or in the buildup of attitudes within each community toward the other.

There are several issues that emerge from Luther's positions toward Jews and Judaism that are worth revisiting from the perspective of lessons that could be applied reciprocally. I would like to draw attention here to four points of theological or ideological nature that are central to Luther's view of Jews and that should serve as food for thought for contemporary Jewish educators and thinkers.

THE QUESTION OF THE LEGITIMACY OF THE OTHER FAITH

In theoretical terms, the most fundamental issue that shapes relations negatively and that informs various expressions of a negative attitude to the other is the sense of the illegitimacy of the other faith. For Luther, Judaism is not valid. It has ceased being a viable spiritual option. The question remains what to do with the Jews, and Luther's career in relation to the Jews covers a range of options. Yet, what is common to the entire spectrum is the fundamental assumption that Judaism as such is not a valid religious option.

Of course, Luther did not invent this position, but he may have perfected it or its applications and consequences. Moreover, the place that Jews and Judaism occupied in his thinking is possibly unparalleled. Consequently, the question of legitimacy and recognition is the theoretical foundation stone of one of the most central issues with which Luther struggled, and its consequences are extreme.

Luther does not hold the copyright to undermining the very legitimacy of another religion. The negativity that he encountered in Jewish attitudes to Christianity is also argued, in theoretical terms, on the same basis.[19] Many, perhaps most, of the Jews in his time,[20] as well as a significant number of contemporary Jewish faithful, would reciprocate Luther's attitude. Luther is an invitation for a Jewish audience to consider how harmful such an approach is, regardless of how justified it may seem to believers on whatever the appropriate internal grounds are. To argue that another religion is not legitimate or viable or effective is a form of violence and can ultimately lead to concrete expressions of violence.

Let me cite Jaroslav Pelikan on how central recognition is to advancing relations between Jews and Luther's followers:

> Without minimizing the seriousness of any of [the factors offered for Luther on the Jews], I cannot escape the conviction that the time has come for those who study Luther and admire him to acknowledge, more unequivocally and less pugnaciously than they have, that on this issue Luther's thought and language are simply beyond defense. But any such acknowledgement must be based, theologically, on a much more fundamental conviction, namely, that Judaism is not, as Luther and the centuries before him maintained, a "shadow" destined to

19. For a discussion of fundamental approaches of a Jewish theology of religion to other religions, and for consideration of legitimacy of other religions, as well as of how the notion of idolatry makes another religion illegitimate, see Alon Goshen-Gottstein, "Towards a Jewish Theology of World Religions: Framing the Issues," in *Jewish Theology and World Religions*, ed. Alon Goshen-Gottstein and Eugene Korn (Oxford: Littman Library of Jewish Civilization, 2012), 7–20.

20. The majority of the opinions holding that Christianity is not idolatrous are later than Luther, even though the great codifier R. Yosef Karo, who was a contemporary of Luther, also held this view. See Eugene Korn, "Rethinking Christianity: Rabbinic Positions and Possibilities," in *Jewish Theology and World Religions*, ed. Alon Goshen-Gottstein and Eugene Korn (Oxford: Littman Library of Jewish Civilization, 2012), 197n27.

> disappear with the coming of Christianity, even though it stubbornly held on to its existence, but a permanent part of the wondrous dispensation of God in human history. I do not pretend to know with any finality what this implies for the Christian view of revelation, or for the Christian doctrine of Jesus Christ. But I am sure that this generation of Christians and Jews is obliged to look again at the issues that divide them. Christians cannot evade the problem of the continuing validity and unique witness of Israel and Jews cannot continue to treat as a mere upstart a movement that embodies some of the central insights of the Hebrew Bible. And if this is so, then today it will have to be here in the new world that the two confront each other: a new Judaism, chastened by the holocaust and revived by a new entry into the promised land; and a Christianity, hopefully also chastened and revived by these enormous historical realities, a Christianity in which the voice of Luther is both completed and privileged to speak with special fervor.[21]

It is actually only a small step from denying legitimacy to envisioning the disappearance of the party that lacks such legitimacy. That Luther would wish Jews would disappear from the Christian environment (though not be physically annihilated) is a direct consequence of the lack of legitimacy of Judaism. Jews, perhaps I should say some Jews, have manifested a similar desire as part of their messianic vision.[22] Deprived of the power to make recommendations to state authorities as Luther could, they projected the same attitude to an ideal future, captured in prayers and in the workings of the religious imagination.

Luther criticizes a Jewish understanding of election that leaves no room for others, in fact setting up a distinction between the chosen and the damned. If they claim salvation

21. Jaroslav Pelikan, "Luther Comes to the New World," in *Luther and the Dawn of the Modern Era*, ed. Heiko A. Oberman (Leiden: Brill, 1974), 9.

22. See Israel Jacob Yuval, *Two Nations in Your Womb: Perceptions of Jews and Christians in Late Antiquity and the Middle Ages* (Berkeley: University of California Press, 2006), chapter 3.

for themselves, then in fact they despise the rest of humanity.[23] It might be helpful here to distinguish between positions—that is, philosophically established or otherwise accepted tenets of faith—and attitudes that describe common perspective, popular opinion, and read the pulse of a religious community in relation to another. Philosophically or theologically, one can't say Luther is right. This is not a philosophically defensible understanding of Jewish election.[24] Yet, Luther raises a challenge that is, to this very day and perhaps especially today, one of the greatest challenges of Jewish theology. What is the meaning of Jewish election and its purpose, and how does it relate to the standing of the rest of humanity?[25] Luther's critique picks up on a real issue that continues to challenge Jewish thought and the Jewish community. If this idea contributed to negative attitudes to the other, then we must consider Luther a mirror, surely one of many, by means of which this question is refracted back to us, as a challenge and an invitation to revisit the price of election and exclusivism in the presence and in full awareness of the other.

23. Brooks Schramm, "Introduction: Martin Luther, the Bible and the Jewish People," in *Martin Luther, the Bible, and the Jewish People: A Reader*, ed. Brooks Schramm and Kirsi I. Stjerna (Minneapolis: Fortress Press, 2012), 7.

24. For a range of understandings of Jewish election, see the following resources: Michael Wyschogrod, *The Body of Faith: Judaism as Corporeal Election* (New York: Seabury, 1983); Menachem Marc Kellner, *Maimonides on Judaism and the Jewish People* (Albany: State University of New York Press, 1991); David Novak, *The Election of Israel: The Idea of the Chosen People* (Cambridge: Cambridge University Press, 1995); Reuven Firestone, *Who Are the Real Chosen People: The Meaning of Chosenness in Judaism, Christianity and Islam* (Woodstock, VT: Skylight Paths, 2008); Jerome (Yehuda) Gellman, *God's Kindness Has Overwhelmed Us: A Contemporary Doctrine of the Jews as the Chosen People* (Boston: Academic Studies Press, 2013).

25. See Goshen-Gottstein, "Towards a Jewish Theology," 3–6.

Chosenness need not imply that the nonchosen are illegitimate. There are important understandings that would prevent such a conclusion.[26] Yet one cannot deny that some Jews, including important ones, do identify election with lack of value of others. If validation of the other is fundamental to the theoretical and theological attitude to the other, Luther drives home, in a conscious way, a question that is fundamental to Judaism's relations with others. It is a question that cannot be ignored, even if it was posed by someone who in the process enacted the same dynamics in the reverse, with horrendous consequences in real life.

Election is not the only basis for denying legitimacy to the other. There are other drives and questions that can yield the same result. Challenges that are too great may produce a facile answer that does away with the other, either in terms of legitimacy or in terms of imagined reality. One may recognize a parallel dynamic. First, there is a theological or metaphysical question that must be resolved. For Luther, it is how to understand Jewish refusal to recognize Christ. The answer leads to the demonization of Jews and ultimately to despair that can only be addressed through recommendations of exiling Jews from Christian countries.[27] For some Jews, it is to understand how it is possible for non-Jews to fail to recognize the true God and to torment and persecute his people. The response is to postpone vindication to a future time and to ultimately eliminate all opponents in the imagined pure and perfected world of the future.[28]

26. These include notions of degrees of commandment and election, such as through the seven Noachian commandments, instrumentality toward the welfare of others, parallel relationships with the divine, and affirmation of the simultaneity of humanity being created in the divine image and special relationship entrusted to the people of Israel.

27. See Schramm, "Introduction: Martin Luther," 5–6.

28. See Yuval, *Two Nations*, chapter 3.

Recognizing the parallel dynamic leads us to consider how human and understandable the response is, and yet how much it does not accord with a higher view of God and the ideal relations between religions. It takes a higher vision, a God's-eye vision, that is based on love to be able to contain the suffering, the paradox, and what can't be understood in the continued existence of the other. Such may be the vision of a "religious genius," and in this sense neither Luther nor Jews who held reciprocal views were able to rise to such a perspective.

THE CHARGE OF IDOLATRY

Claiming for Jews an association with the devil means, in fact, that the Jews have lost their relationship with God. In other words, they become attached to another power. This is, then, a claim that Jews are idolaters who do not worship the true God. The charge of idolatry is fundamental to delegitimation. We worship God; you worship another.

It is interesting that Luther cites the story of the golden calf to justify the burning of synagogues.[29] Similarly, Luther charges Jews with the practice of magic as a dimension of idolatrous practices.[30]

The Jewish category of *Avoda Zara* is founded on othering.[31] The term connotes strange or foreign god and relates to an "other" god, whose worshippers are similarly othered in the process. This is the most fundamental prism through

29. Martin Luther, *D. Martin Luthers Werke*, 127 vols. (Weimar: H. Böhlau, 1883–2009), 53:541. See Kaufmann, *Luther's Jews*, 115.

30. Kaufmann, *Luther's Jews*, 79. See further R. Po-chia Hsia, *The Myth of Ritual Murder: Jews and Magic in Reformation Germany* (New Haven: Yale University Press, 1988).

31. See Alon Goshen-Gottstein, *Same God, Other god: Judaism, Hinduism, and the Problem of Idolatry* (New York: Palgrave Macmillan, 2015), 27–31.

which Judaism looks at world religions. They are either *Avoda Zara* or not. Christianity has been seen primarily through the lens of foreign god and foreign worship, relating to the worship of Jesus, the notion of the Trinity, and the worship of images. Varying halakic positions seek to affirm Christianity's legitimacy despite the appearance of worshipping another god.[32] The debate goes on, and the arson attack on the church at Tabgha is one contemporary example of how practical consequences can be drawn from one specific position.

What is fascinating in reading Luther's views of Jews is how reciprocal the charge of idolatry can be in the process of mutual delegitimation. Jews typically think that they alone are in the position of sitting in judgment over non-pure monotheists. It never occurs to them that the charge, and the deeper relational dynamics, can be reciprocal. It is precisely this reciprocity that invites us to consider the implications of the very charge of *Avoda Zara*. From Luther, we see that we have been victims of the application of the way of thinking that the category embodies.

The charge of idolatry is one that has moral consequences. We come to recognize that it is only a step from affirming the otherness of another god to taking up harmful activities toward the other as an extension of this theological position. The potential distinction between religious/theoretical position and practical/moral consequences cannot withstand the forces of political power and the vicissitudes of historical change. When this view is coupled with power, the move from the theoretical position to its moral consequences is readily crossed.

If at the root of the charge of idolatry is a view that empha-

32. See Korn, "Rethinking Christianity."

sizes the distinction between self and other, in fact we discover that a dualistic worldview lurks behind the charge of idolatry or can readily be seen as its foundation and extension. This dualistic worldview characterizes Luther's view of enemies, Jews and non-Jews. It is also a central component of kabbalistic thinking, but more broadly of the orientation of significant sections of classical Judaism.

What are the implications of the recognition that dualistic organization of one's worldview and its application is a characteristic of some Jewish worldviews as well as the worldviews of some religious groups and thinkers that have led to Jewish suffering and persecution? It is certainly an invitation to reconsider the broader consequences of dualistic thinking. It may not be grounds for rejecting it. From a dualistic perspective, the attacks on Jews could be presented as indications of the "other side." Whether the attacks are ideological or practical, the power that reveals itself through them may be identified as a dark force, the very demonic force that Luther charges Jews of associating with. If we consider morality rather than theology as a yardstick for recognizing other spiritual forces,[33] then the horrors perpetrated in the name of one religion against another would be demonic expressions. While this could reinforce the view of the other as associated with "non-god," we must recognize that the argument has to work both ways. In other words, if we are to argue that harmful moral consequences of othering are in fact expressions of metaphysical otherness, we must be willing to acknowledge the same when such expressions are found within "our" religion. Thc distinction between divine and nondivine then cuts across the borderlines of distinct religions. If so, we come back full circle to the realization that

33. See Goshen-Gottstein, *Same God, Other god*, 189–92.

dualistic thought can produce harmful consequences in any tradition. At the very least, this is an invitation to examine the internal checks and balances that religious traditions contain regarding their potential to become violent in relation to one another.

There is another perspective worth noting regarding Luther and idolatry. It has more to do with theology than with metaphysics. Some Lutheran thinkers who have considered Luther in view of his attitude to the Jews have touched upon the problem of his own theology. It is common to recognize that his "theology of the cross" has given way to "a theology of glory" in relation to the Jews. This has prompted one scholar to speak of this move in terms of idolatry. The claim that Luther holds the keys to correct understanding of the divine intention is to be considered idolatrous. Idolatry can be helpful in distancing oneself from the historical positions toward the Jews taken by the Reformer. It is not him that one adores but rather the true teachings that he pointed to. To uphold him as perfect, and therefore to also accept the negative teachings he offered, is tantamount to idolatry.[34]

THE TRUTH OF SCRIPTURE AND THE CERTITUDE OF KNOWLEDGE

This latter point opens up to another important issue that arises from Luther's views on the Jews. Luther's views are the consequences of serious reading of Scripture and insistence

34. Eric W. Gritsch, "Luther and the Jews: Toward a Judgment of History," in *Stepping-Stones to Further Jewish-Lutheran Relationships*, ed. Harold H. Ditmanson (Minneapolis: Augsburg, 1990), 116. Another Lutheran author has described the core of Luther's theology in relation to Judaism, and its relationship to Jesus, as "an idolatry of Jesus." See Aarne Siirala, "Reflections from a Lutheran Perspective," in *Auschwitz: Beginning of New Era? Reflections on the Holocaust*, ed. Eva Fleischner (New York: Ktav, 1977), 142.

on a correct reading of Scripture. Had Luther not been professor of Old Testament, he would likely never have reached the conclusions he did in relation to the Jews. These grow out of a particular interpretation that insists on reading the Old Testament in light of the New and that has no room for alternative readings. Luther presents us with a challenge that is fundamental to the encounter between traditions today. Luther's modality is representative of much of classical religion. Scripture dictates policy, and we hold the correct key to its interpretation. It requires the rise of a parallel commanding reality—that of morality or human rights or the needs of contemporary religious coexistence—and it is only in view of the horrors that can be inflicted as a consequence of the unbridled application of a view of Scripture to reality that religions begin to confront the challenge of how to deal with difficult texts. How to recognize multiple interpretations? How to balance faithfulness to scriptural tradition with a moral sensibility that is sensitive to the harmful consequences of particular readings?

The implications of this balancing of moral and scriptural perspectives are a different kind of hermeneutic, less self-confident, more open to self-criticism, even to doubt, and cognizant of multiple interpretations of one's own formative texts. This hermeneutical "revolution" is relevant for all religions whose texts contain expressions of violence that can be applied to other religions and their members. It is particularly relevant in today's world in Islamic hermeneutics, but remains relevant for Jews and Christians as they delve into the sources of their tradition in an attempt to justify religious pluralism and to keep the potential for religious violence in check.[35] In all this, Luther can serve as a symbol for a

35. For one example within a growing field of literature, see Alon Goshen-

challenge, possibly a malady, that all religious traditions partake of.

The question of interpretation is closely related to the sense that one possesses truth. Luther was convinced of the correctness of his interpretation to a very high degree.[36] Accordingly, he was informed by a sense of truth. Luther's sense of being in possession of biblical truth had direct consequences in terms of pressure on Jews.[37]

> In matters of belief, as distinct from matters of Christian love, Luther insisted there could be no leniency, for the authority of God's word was at stake.[38]

Love and truth are juxtaposed. Truth has its own claims that seem to trump those of love. Historical perspective of the wrongs that a sense of fullness of truth can bring about in relation to others forces us to question whether a more humble approach, or an alternative approach, to truth is not required.[39] If truth is the central value to emerge from our "knowledge" of scripture and religious tradition, a consideration of historical consequences of consistent and extreme application of this approach leads us to wonder whether religions should not cultivate the alternative hermeneutic, a hermeneutic of love.

Gottstein, ed., *The Religious Other: Hostility, Hospitality and the Hope of Human Flourishing* (Lanham, MD: Lexington, 2015).

36. Kaufmann, *Luther's Jews*, 63.

37. Kaufmann, *Luther's Jews*, p. 63.

38. Kaufmann, *Luther's Jews*, 88.

39. On rethinking the notion of truth from a Jewish perspective see Goshen-Gottstein, "Towards a Jewish Theology," 20–33. I am presently preparing for publication a volume, scheduled to appear at Lexington Books, that brings together Jewish voices that seek to articulate an understanding of "truth" within the framework of a Jewish theology of religions.

READING JEWISH HISTORY AND EXILE

One of the important arguments that Luther put forward in relation to the Jews has to do with continuing Jewish exile. Luther could not imagine that God would still be with the Jews following 1,500 years of exile.

> Luther was also familiar with Jewish prayers that impressed him by their religious nature. "I would give gold chalices worth 200 florins if I could pray as they pray." But it was precisely the fervour and expressive power of Jewish prayers that raised for him even more urgently the issue of their ineffectiveness. His amazement that God could leave such prayers unheard, that he was "silent," could be explained only by his "great and inexpressible anger" that had been upon the Jews now for 1,500 years.[40]

We are at a point in time that allows us to revisit this approach. A contemporary reevaluation of Luther takes on very different meaning when conducted from a perspective that may reasonably be interpreted as a significant change in the very historical reality that Luther appealed to as proof of Jews having been rejected by God.

Looking at it from some distance, can one fault Luther for interpreting historical reality as he did? Could he really be expected to enter into the depth of Jewish faithfulness despite the depth of historical suffering? Luther was caught up in his own world of faith, and his faith left little room for recognizing that the Jewish experience that he marshalled as support for his own theological views was in fact an expression of deep faith. Perhaps if that was realized, a more pluralistic approach to the faith of the other could have emerged. It is a mandate of today to approach faith as a phenomenon

40. Kaufmann, *Luther's Jews*, 99.

and to recognize its power, independently of positions taken and their reasonability.[41] The depth of faith as a human spiritual phenomenon is itself testimony to the presence of the Divine, independent of argued theological positions.[42] But this is a hard-won insight, and we cannot expect Luther to have attained it. Perhaps it required a greater spiritual vision than he could muster, informed as he was by a sense of Scripture and its correct interpretation.

Obviously, a turn in history for the Jews does not resolve the discussion between Luther and the Jews. It is not as if at the time he had the upper hand and now Jews do, having been vindicated in history. Rather, it is a call to more careful application of history as a yardstick of interpretation of divine will and reality, and a call to establish other criteria—more human, moral, and experiential—to recognize the presence of God amongst humans. The application of such criteria is equally significant for the possibility of Jews recognizing traces of divine life in Christian spiritual life as it is for the demand that Christians find this in Jewish spiritual life.[43]

Revisiting religious relations through the testimony of Luther and "what went wrong" is in many ways a call to humility with reference to truth, to the other, to various absolutes. One of the dimensions of this call for humility is also a call for Jewish humility with reference to a view of Jewish history. Covenantal thinking is a foundation of biblical thought. It certainly includes the possibility of abroga-

41. See Wilfred Cantwell Smith, *Faith and Belief* (Princeton: Princeton University Press, 1979).

42. Wilfred Cantwell Smith, *Towards a World Theology: Faith and the Comparative History of Religion* (London: Macmillan, 1981).

43. See Goshen-Gottstein, *Same God, Other god*, 189–94. See further Alon Goshen-Gottstein, "God between Christians and Jews: Is It the Same God?," in *Do We Worship the Same God? Jews, Christians, and Muslims in Dialogue*, ed. Miroslav Volf (Grand Rapids: Eerdmans, 2012), 50–75.

tion or near abrogation of the covenant and chastising Israel in view of Israel's infidelity to the covenant. Jewish suffering is understood in light of violation of the covenant.[44] Jewish thought has moved since rabbinic times away from covenantal thinking, in part due to the changed historical fate and the need to uphold Jewish existence and its value independently of the violation of the covenant. A return to the homeland and a certain independence has been accompanied by a return to covenantal thinking. From this perspective, we must ask whether Luther was not, in fact, speaking the truth, a truth he could only see in mid-process, lacking the fullness of vision of how it would eventually unfold. Indeed, Jews were chastised for their covenantal violation. And this is just what Luther saw. In fact, he became part of that story, an instrument for further curses for the Jews. For Luther, the story unfolded in a different way, leading to a redefinition of who was the true Israel. But Israel's story has unfolded in a way that affirms the original story line from Israel's perspective. From the perspective of reestablishment in land and in relation to God, we are called to consider a humble approach to the view of past Jewish suffering. Indeed, Jews suffered as part of a greater plan that can be described using covenantal language. An outside observer allows us to recognize this more fully. He does not, however, hold the key to interpreting the story in its fullness.

God could have used Luther's imperfections or intellectual consistency or theological passion to continue applying a regime appropriate for a period of covenantal chastisement. If indeed that time is over, then revisiting Luther in this light allows us to develop greater compassion for the reality of both Jews and their enemies, as all sides play out a divine plan. Part of that divine plan for today may be going beyond the

44. See Leviticus 26 and Deuteronomy 28.

paradigms of that age and establishing new relations between the communities.

6. PROTECTION OF IDENTITY

Identity lies at the core of Jewish-Christian relations. We have noted the question "Who is Israel?" that has overshadowed Christian-Jewish relations for two millennia. We have seen how concerns for Christian identity informed Luther's growing hostility toward Jews. Looking at present-day Jewish-Christian relations, it seems to me that Jews mirror the same concerns and many of the same attitudes that informed Luther's approach to identity, while Christians have shifted significantly in past decades. For Jews, maintaining identity is arguably the supreme cultural value. Faced with physical extinction in the earlier part of the twentieth century, Judaism fights for its survival as it fears spiritual extinction through intermarriage, ignorance, and a move of significant numbers of its people away from core identity-forming dimensions: religion, state, land, community. This is particularly so in diaspora, but is also a serious concern within the State of Israel. This is probably the single greatest concern of Jewish organizations after, or alongside, the concern for ensuring the survival of the State of Israel.

Concern for identity impacts common Jewish views of Christianity. The problem here is that Christianity consists of many groups, and their attitudes to Judaism vary. While Catholics have avoided missionary work toward Jews for decades and have now made it official policy,[45] various Protestant groups missionize actively. Missionary work takes

45. This was articulated recently in the document published by the Pontifical Council for Religious Relations with the Jews, titled *The Gifts and the Calling of God Are Irrevocable*.

place in all places where Jews live and is extensive in the State of Israel. For professionals of the Jewish-Christian encounter, a distinction is maintained between different Christian denominations and their attitude to mission to the Jews. But for most Jews, in particular among the Orthodox, where resistance to recognizing change among Christians is greatest, one cannot name denominations, let alone distinguish between them. Consequently, fear of mission, or in other words the drive to preserve Jewish identity, continues to shape much of Orthodox response to Christianity.

Christians often have a hard time understanding Jewish responses to Christianity and its missionary efforts. Luther is actually a very good bridge. In him we see, and through him Christians can come to appreciate, just how powerfully the missionary drive impacts relations between groups. The practice of mission is seen as a violation of one's most intimate identity. It raises boundaries between communities, even when the winds of time call for the lowering of such boundaries. Coupled with theological ideals and painful historical memories, it becomes a major point of division between traditions.

Identity plays out in even more difficult ways in view of the fact that there are groups that blur the boundaries between the traditions. Various Jewish-Christian messianic groups create further anxiety among the Orthodox. Once again, Luther is helpful in allowing Christians to grasp this. One of Luther's attacks was on the Sabbatarians, who were Christians who took up Jewish practices.[46] The attack on Sabbatarians is intimately linked to Luther's attacks on Judaism. This is the exact mirror image of groups like Jews for Jesus

46. Kaufmann, *Luther's Jews*, 89ff. It is not clear whether Luther was able to distinguish between Christians taking up Jewish practices and Christians becoming Jewish. In terms of threat to identity, the distinction is not all that significant.

and other groups that offer some combination of two religious identities. One result of missionary efforts is to create groups that display elements of dual identity, and as we see this can occur on the Jewish as well as on the Christian side.

I once heard a noted Jewish leader stating that the one thing that all Jewish denominations can agree upon is that messianic Jews are beyond consensus. I do not wish to argue the point in and of itself. But this statement is telling. It suggests that concerns for Jewish identity are so powerful that they serve as the single greatest uniting force across internal Jewish divisions. And these come together when a group seeks to affirm its own religious identity in ways that compromise the authenticity and integrity of Jewish identity, as recognized by most streams of present-day Judaism.

Looking at it from this perspective, one is quite sympathetic to Luther. He responds to whatever he is told of Sabbatarians in ways that are very typical of how Jews continue to respond to various Jewish-Christian groups. In both cases, we note how central affirmation of identity and the quest for authenticity of religious life are.

Having recognized this commonality, one is also challenged as to how to view it in the framework of contemporary attitudes of interreligious opening and tolerance. In fact, many who are tolerant toward other religions adopt intolerant, or highly critical, views when it comes to groups that threaten their identity. It is a fact of note that even Jews who are completely open to Christianity and to Jewish-Christian dialogue remain closed to contact with messianic Jews.

This fact is all the more pronounced when we note how much less insistent some contemporary Christian thinkers are in relation to establishment and maintenance of Christian identity. While for the most part, Christian thinkers and leaders seek to uphold faithfulness to tradition, in line with centuries of faith, we find a range of respected thinkers exploring the boundaries of Christian identity in relation to other faiths. Christians are at the forefront of issues of multiple religious identity.[47] And the interesting thing is that experiments in multiple religious identities are carried out by faithful who often belong to mainline churches.

None of this occurs in present-day Judaism. There are many Jews who are members of other faiths and who continue to self-identity as Jews on ethnic grounds.[48] But we have no noteworthy examples of Jews upholding a model of simultaneous practice of Judaism as a faith alongside another. The most notable examples are various messianic groups, leading us back to the question under discussion.

What does it mean, then, that contemporary Jewish attitudes correspond to Luther's attitudes? If we consider the "Luther model" as a map for recognizing where religion can go wrong, in terms of intergroup relations, does this mean that we must also abandon faithfulness to identity? Would this lead us to adopt a more flexible approach to Jewish identity and to showing less concern for its transmission across generations? I believe this is not a necessary conclusion. I can suggest several factors for why this not the case:

1. Whereas some components of the model would be considered problematic, others become problematic only in the context of the other elements. Absent ignorance, distance, and othering, the quest for maintaining fidelity to communal identity is not a vice that is to be overcome.

47. See Catherine Cornille, ed., *Many Mansions? Multiple Religious Belonging and Christian Identity* (Maryknoll, NY: Orbis, 2002).

48. In the case of Hinduism, see Alon Goshen-Gottstein, *The Jewish Encounter with Hinduism: Wisdom, Spirituality, Identity* (New York: Palgrave Macmillan, 2016), 113–70.

2. There is something qualitatively different in the quest for maintaining identity than in some of the other items discussed above. Identity is central to who we are; ignorance is not. Even theological views typically offer a greater range than one position, as the multiple options of relating to Christianity in terms of idolatry suggest. Identity, by contrast, is much harder to affirm on a scale. Identity makes total demands on a person, and partial identity or partial affiliation is often a cause for worry in terms of the intergenerational transmission of identity.

3. Given how deeply concerns for identity run and how they galvanize other factors into a comprehensive view of the other, the model under discussion, we are invited to consider whether there is a way of affirming identity that is less exclusionary of individual religious choices that fall outside classical boundaries. Given the prominence of identity maintenance for the global Jewish agenda, whether religious, ethnic, or national, and given the pervasive concern (even fear) of mission to the Jews, it is hard to cultivate a more accepting view of individual choices of either converts to another religion or of attempts at redefining identity so that it is composed of elements of more than one religion. Yet, the broader movements that affect the Jewish world, including secularization, globalization, and indeed the opening up to interreligious relations, do raise the question of whether dialogue can be extended to groups that practice multiple religious identities and whether there is a way of relating to them that is more in line with the attitudes of dialogue and less in continuity with the rejection of the classical model, represented by Luther as well as by most contemporary Jewry. I believe this remains a pastoral challenge that could take a long time to work out. Effectively, entire communities have been written

out of Jewish communal life and consciousness because they have chosen the "Sabbatarian" option. It may be that this is a necessary response in view of the tortuous and painful Jewish history of contact with missionizing religions. Or it may be that a more objective look at dynamics of construction of identity and changing realities within Judaism and between religions will amount to an invitation to revisit how to dialogue or otherwise relate to such groups, without undermining the concerns for Jewish identity.[49]

7. THE APOCALYPTIC DIMENSION

Some scholars consider that some of the extreme positions taken by Luther are a result of an apocalyptic consciousness. Luther was fighting the last battle. The last battle heightened tensions between Christians and others, and his attacks on the Jews, including his deviating from some of his own theological principles, are to be considered in such a context.

While the apocalyptic dimension, per se, is not central to a contemporary Jewish view, the strong messianic dimension that some Jewish groups associate with contemporary Israel and its political realities is. Noteworthy are the extremists, again: an extreme fringe phenomenon that is responsible for the Tabgha arson. Their ideology was to precipitate religious warfare and thereby to hasten a messianic/apocalyptic moment.[50] Theirs was not simply an expression of hate

49. In addition to my discussion in *The Jewish Encounter with Hinduism* cited above, see also pp. 31–38 of the same work, as well as a forthcoming study on Sarmad the Jew. Messianic Jews are the most contentious instance of this phenomenon on the Jewish side, typically shunned by all Jewish denominations. Mark Kinzer, a thoughtful and learned member of that community, seeks to cultivate a more academic and open-minded investigation of parameters of multiple religious belonging and identity construction as it relates to this test case.

50. Chaim Levinson, "Meet the Jewish Extremist Group That Seeks to Violently Topple the State," *Haaretz*, August 7, 2015, http://tinyurl.com/y73zl4m4.

against Christians. Rather, acts of vandalism and hate geared at Christians, as well as Muslims, were part of an attempt to subvert the social and political order in order to inaugurate a new era, the kingdom of Israel or the kingdom of God, identified with one another.

Aarne Siirala has written on how Luther's approach to other religions has become ideology.[51] It is precisely, he argues, in the context of an apocalyptic view that theology can become ideology. It is religion as ideology that becomes dualistic and heightens exclusion of certain groups and negative practices toward them. I believe this analysis describes aptly what happened in the fringe circles of Jewish extremists, and what happens to lesser extent in many contemporary Orthodox views of the State of Israel and its global positioning and their views of other faiths. Interpreting a political reality can readily transform theology into ideology, along with the various negative consequences.

The messianic/apocalyptic dimension cannot function independently. It is a magnifying glass that is placed upon the other elements in the "Luther model." This magnifying glass, focused in a particular way, can lead to a conflagration that involves all these elements. It is therefore a dimension that must be recognized as one more factor in a web of factors that can lead to religion going "wrong."

The apocalyptic/messianic dimension also impacts relations on the ground between religions. How one imagines the eschaton is how one will live one's life and one's relations to the other. I have already mentioned Israel Yuval's work on opposing models of messianic expectations. On the one hand, a conversionary model, where non-Jews, enemies, and others will convert and return to Judaism. On the other hand, a

51. Siirala, "Reflections," 141ff.

model that imagines their eventual disappearance as good triumphs over evil, a model Luther is likely to have felt comfortable with. This latter model remains in the literature and can therefore continue to shape attitudes of religious. That Israel remains embattled on multiple fronts—military, religious, international public opinion, international bodies and their approach to Israel—all heightens a sense of isolation and the refuge and consolation that a messianic/eschatological vision can hold. Living in what are for many messianic times can therefore play a dual role in a Jewish approach to other religions. It can open Judaism up to an inclusive messianic spirit or close it up in an embattled, and fundamentally dualistic, mentality.

Is Luther of any help here? One cannot simply dismiss the messianic element out of religious consciousness because it amplifies tensions and brings out what we consider problematic aspects of religion. Perhaps, as in the previous point with reference to identity, the challenge of history is to consider how to uphold certain ideals while not being drawn into the narrowness, otherness, and duality that is often associated with them. In the battle between conflicting messianisms, a look at how apocalyptic views of others has played out negatively in relation to us could be a reminder of the kind of messianism we would wish to practice.

In the case of Israel, this ties to another dimension that can be learned from Luther. Luther was a powerful voice in his day. Much of his power lay in the fact that he had the ear of local princes and state authorities. While he did not have a state that practiced his teachings, his teaching of two kingdoms allowed for a religious infusion within stately affairs, even as it gave these their own sphere of autonomy.

In the case of Judaism, we are faced for the first time with the opportunities provided by a Jewish state. These come with all the accoutrements of state power, including military and other forms of power. One of the lessons from the history of Luther's reception history is precisely to keep apart the teachings of religion from state machinery, inasmuch as it has often played out for the worse, in the case of Jews. Perhaps these lessons need to be heard with particular force on the Jewish side, where state power can be coupled by some (though not necessarily the state itself) with messianic vision and a view that seeks to destroy the other.

For the most part, we might feel justified in taking pride in the words of a Christian playwright *not* having been fulfilled once Jews have come into their own political right. A fifteenth-century play portrays a Christian making the following statement to a Jew: "If you had power over us, as we had in our day over you, after a year not a single Christian would remain alive."[52] Fortunately, the overall balance and tenor of Christian-Jewish relations has changed significantly, as have international norms of treating religious minorities. Still, the traditional texts and attitudes remain part of tradition and therefore have the potential to continue to condition attitudes, resulting in concrete behavior, even if on the periphery, carried out by a small minority.

52. Yuval, *Two Nations*, 133.

Conclusion

In this work, I have attempted to move a discussion of "Luther and the Jews," pitched pointedly as "Luther the Anti-Semite," beyond the historical verdict and judgment of Luther and his historical role. I have also attempted to approach the discussion from a perspective that is other than the victim's perspective. I have sought to integrate significant theological and historical dimensions that characterize Luther's personal attitude and theological position into a broader framework that I called "the Luther model." By means of this model, I have attempted to make a discussion of Luther's imperfections not only a call for Christian repentance and theological self-examination but an invitation for Jews, Christians, and people of all faiths to consider the factors and circumstances under which religion goes wrong—in other words, how and when religion leads to the kind of violent, hateful approach to the other that is the opposite of other core tenets of the faith and orientating principles of its spirituality that we deem to be primary and most defining of our religions, and those aspects that today's world is most in need of. Because of our value judgments, significantly different than those from those of Luther and most of his contemporaries, and because of what we expect of religion, all religions, globally, we have an obligation to study the factors that make religion go wrong. The life of a great religious personality is accordingly studied as a model for how and when religion goes wrong.

In this exercise we are aided by the "Luther model." Its importance is that it invites us to look in a mirror. Mirrors, as we have seen, are fundamental to a Jewish conversation on Luther. It seems Luther could not see the Jews, just as many contemporary Jews cannot see Christians. One has a hard time looking at oneself in a critical way. Recognizing that someone who has been considered an enemy actually manifests the same traits and brings together an entire set of characteristics that add up to an approach to the other that one can find within oneself is one way of gaining critical distance from oneself. If Jews, some Jews, can look at Luther and see something of themselves, or at least if they can be challenged to examine what fundamental dynamics cut across religious difference and offer a commonality of where religion can go wrong, then Luther can serve as a great teacher. Surely, he intended to be a teacher of a different kind of truth, a saving truth, a truth of love. But perhaps the path to offering a teaching of true love passes through recognition of the faults of the teacher. It is more than a case of an example not to follow. It is the recognition that in looking at Luther we may in fact be looking at something that exists in us. If we can adopt such a view, then we can not only view the Reformer with greater compassion, recognizing our imperfections in his, we can discover in him the very common human misery, imperfection, and limitation that calls for God's grace, a grace needed by both Jews and Christians.